Contents

Part 1

Introduction

Shakespeare: the person: 'Gentle Will'

When 'gentle' William Shakespeare died on 23 April 1616 he left no diary; so only from his poems and his plays, published by friends seven years later, and from a few printed comments and public records of that time, can we learn about the man.

We know that he received the free school education normal for the son of a respectable middle-class father, who had him baptised at Stratford-upon-Avon on 26 April 1564.

He was the eldest boy, with seven sisters and brothers, growing up in a busy, well-to-do household, the father of which, John Shakespeare, was a glove-maker and also a public figure in the town. He became mayor in 1568 when William was four. The mother was Mary Arden, from an important local family who were Roman Catholic. But by the time Will was thirteen years old the family's fortunes had sunk so low that the town council had to contribute towards the·cost of their seven-year-old daughter's funeral, and three years later John Shakespeare was fined for not attending church. In 1586 he ceased to be an alderman. So, before and during his schooling, the boy William must have shared in births and deaths, the reduction of living standards resulting from his father's fall from power and his unsuccessful struggle with the state authorities over religion.

His formal education in Latin grammar was rigorous, and from the classical texts and translations he learnt Roman history, rhetoric and the technicalities of verse and drama-making; and in Ovid he found the strange tales of the myths of Greece and Rome. On being withdrawn from school he may have earned money, it has been suggested, as a tutor or even a lawyer's clerk or both, for like his father he was socially ambitious.

On 28 November 1582, when he was only eighteen, he married Anne Hathaway, who was eight years older, and she bore him a daughter, Susannah, six months later. With the arrival in 1585 of twins Hamnet and Judith the responsibilities and problems of the young family man increased.

So by the age of twenty-one Shakespeare already had a keen experience of the pleasures and pains of life in the country, as a lover, husband and father. He had probably seen, and been impressed by, the exciting theatrical performances put on by the visiting players, particularly those of the Queen's Men, and the leading professional actor of the time, Edward Alleyn, during the 1580s. It is not known when Shakespeare went to London, but by 1592 he had been there long enough to attract attention and envy, as a non-university man, by his growing reputation for acting and writing. The playwright Robert Greene bitterly refers to him, in that year, as an 'upstart crow . . . in his own conceit the only Shakescene in the country'. He must have learnt quickly how to practise his craft in the theatre for his popularity to provoke such criticism.

The next year, however, the theatres were closed because of the

THE GLOBE PLAYHOUSE

The theatre, originally built by James Burbage in 1576, was made of wood (Burbage had been trained as a carpenter). It was situated to the north of the River Thames on Shoreditch in Finsbury Fields. There was trouble with the lease of the land, and so the theatre was dismantled in 1598, and reconstructed 'in another forme' on the south side of the Thames as the Globe. Its sign is thought to have been a figure of the Greek hero Hercules carrying the globe. It was built in six months, its galleries being roofed with thatch. This caught fire in 1613 when some smouldering wadding, from a cannon used in a performance of Shakespeare's *Henry VIII*, lodged in it. The theatre was burnt down, and when it was rebuilt again on the old foundations, the galleries were roofed with tiles.

YORK NOTES

General Editors: Professor A.N. Jeffares *(University*

**This book is to be returned on or before
the last date stamped below.**

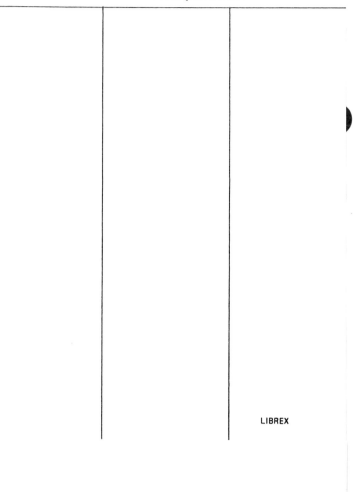

LIBREX

The Illustrations of The Globe Playhouse are from
The Globe Restored in Theatre: A Way of Seeing by
Walter C. Hodges, published by Oxford University
Press. © Oxford University Press

YORK PRESS
Immeuble Esseily, Place Riad Solh, Beirut.

LONGMAN GROUP UK LIMITED
Longman House, Burnt Mill, Harlow,
Essex CM20 2JE, England
Associated companies, branches and representatives
throughout the world

© Librairie du Liban 1980

First published 1980
Sixteenth impression 1993

ISBN 0-582-02256-8

Produced by Longman Singapore Publishers Pte Ltd
Printed in Singapore

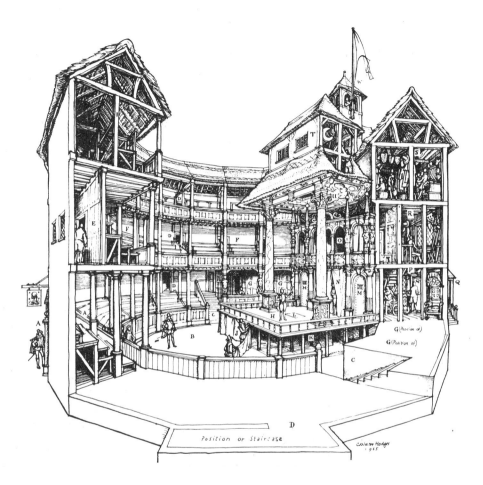

A CONJECTURAL RECONSTRUCTION OF THE INTERIOR OF
THE GLOBE PLAYHOUSE

AA Main entrance
 B The Yard
CC Entrances to lowest gallery
 D Entrance to staircase and upper galleries
 E Corridor serving the different sections of the middle gallery
 F Middle gallery ('Twopenny Rooms')
 G 'Gentlemen's Rooms' or Lords' Rooms'
 H The stage
 J The hanging being put up round the stage
 K The 'Hell' under the stage
 L The stage trap, leading down to the Hell
MM Stage doors

 N Curtained 'place behind the stage'
 O Gallery above the stage, used as required sometimes by musicians, sometimes by spectators, and often as part of the play
 P Back-stage area (the tiring-house)
 Q Tiring-house door
 R Dressing-rooms
 S Wardrobe and storage
 T The hut housing the machine for lowering enthroned gods, etc., to the stage
 U The 'Heavens'
 W Hoisting the playhouse flag

plague, but Shakespeare enchanted London by his two long poems *Venus and Adonis* and *The Rape of Lucrece*, both dedicated to the Earl of Southampton, who became his patron. Shakespeare was now famous, and when the theatres reopened in 1594 he became a shareholding member of the Lord Chamberlain's Company, one of the two top acting groups in the country. So, as the new, popular plays flowed each year from his pen, Shakespeare as a partner in the Globe Theatre now became prosperous. But the family's joy at the award to them of a coat of arms in 1596 was darkened by the death of Will's son Hamnet. The following year, however, with a shrewd view to his retirement, he bought New Place, the largest available house in Stratford.

There were more sorrows for the maturing dramatist with his father's death in 1601, his brother's in 1608, and perhaps the unauthorised publication in 1609 of his *Sonnets*. These were the years when the great tragedies were written, of which *Antony and Cleopatra* and *Coriolanus* were the last. With shares also in the new indoor Blackfriars Theatre in 1609 his wealth and fame increased so much that in 1611 he could now give up London and active work in the theatre itself and return to his wife and daughters at Stratford, before he was fifty. But he continued to write, and may have revisited London to see his final plays performed at the Blackfriars Theatre, near which he bought a house in 1613. His daughter Susannah had married Dr John Hall in 1607, and in 1616 the younger girl married also, only two months before Shakespeare was buried on 25 April.

His grave in Stratford church is now a place of pilgrimage for thousands of visitors every year. The painted bust above his tomb, though perhaps a likeness, is not inspiring, but the Chandos portrait shows the broad forehead from which the full hair behind has receded, beard, moustache and a golden ring in his left ear. The 'honest', 'open' eyes above firm lips parting at the start of a smile, give us the feeling of the 'excellent phantasy', 'brave notions' and, above all, 'gentle expressions', which Ben Jonson affectionately attributed to his 'beloved' friend.

The poet: 'Sweet Swan of Avon'

The Elizabethan term 'poet' meant playwright as well, for although Shakespeare first acquired fame as a maker of verses it is the poetry of his plays that has made them endure. The poems consist of the two long narratives of *Venus and Adonis* and *The Rape of Lucrece*, the shorter *The Phoenix and the Turtle*, and the 154 *Sonnets*. Few readers except scholars today do more than dip into the long poems, which are interesting as Shakespeare's earliest public efforts; but the entire sequence of the *Sonnets* still makes magnificent reading, giving great pleasure and satisfaction. Evidence is not conclusive for us to know whether these love poems describe Shakespeare's intense emotional feelings for a boy and later for a woman, or instead are brilliant verbal exercises making fun of the contemporary sonneteers and their stylised affectations.

However, it is not only Shakespeare's skilful employment of words that astonishes us as we read—his vocabulary consists of more than 30,000 words—but the imaginative genius which transforms everyday, universal emotions and objects into an experience of lyrical beauty. Somehow, always, the right word is used at the right moment. Shakespeare went on from these poems to drama, taking with him this gift for words which is shown clearly in his early plays, such as *Love's Labour's Lost* and *Romeo and Juliet*. He was not consciously creating literary English but spontaneously giving freedom to his 'muse of fire' (*Henry V* I.1), singing out the popular language in which he thought and felt, and in which he expressed himself. He boldly took the stiff, lumpy blank verse of the day and changed it into elegant dramatic poetry. His mastery of the medium made his lines, and hence his plays come convincingly alive. Think of a page of Shakespeare's verse as a piece of textile, the horizontal threads being the lines of words, the vertical ones being the unprinted pause divisions between each foot of the rhythm. The lines consist of five feet each of short-long stressed beats, distributed along the syllables of the words of differing lengths, which make up the line:

$$\overset{\cup}{\text{The}} \overset{—}{\text{barge}} / \overset{\cup}{\text{she}} \overset{—}{\text{sat}} / \overset{\cup}{\text{in}} \overset{—}{\text{like}} / \overset{\cup}{\text{a}} \overset{—}{\text{burn}}/\overset{\cup}{\text{ished}} \overset{—}{\text{throne,}}$$

This is an iambic pentameter, a verse line of five (pente) measures (feet) of two syllables (iambs). So Sonnet 18:

$$\overset{\cup}{\text{Shall}} \overset{—}{\text{I}} / \overset{\cup}{\text{com}}\overset{—}{\text{pare}} / \overset{\cup}{\text{thee}} \overset{—}{\text{to}} / \overset{\cup}{\text{a}} \overset{—}{\text{sum}}/\overset{\cup}{\text{mer's}} \overset{—}{\text{day?}}$$

This, to use a musical metaphor, is the pattern of notes upon which the poet-dramatist improvises his verbal melodies. Shakespeare did not permit himself to be limited by rules of grammar or spelling. He compressed or extended, beheaded or curtailed, joined and even created entirely new words, according to the immediate needs of his meanings and rhythm, within the framework of the pentameter. But we, studying the play, must remember all the time that the words, written to be spoken, must be sounded as well as seen. The 'infinite variety' of the speeches (plays are entirely composed of speeches) is obtained by the poet's manipulation of his words, whose particular order, with their strong and unstressed syllables, will produce the rhythmic pattern required to suit the character, mood and intentions of the person who is speaking them. Shakespeare's outstanding skill was in his creation of new metaphors, similes, and deeply evocative imagery in the unexpected newness of the phrases used to communicate his ideas and emotions, through his characters.

The player and the playwright: 'Mr Shakescene'

Shakespeare achieved thirty-seven plays, an average of one every six months for nearly twenty years. He wrote as an actor-poet to provide not literary masterpieces for publication but popular and topical entertainments, suitable for the skills of the performers around him in his company, which was largely cooperative. It was not until 1623 that the plays were published together in one volume, by two of Shakespeare's friends, John Hemmings and Henry Condell, partners in the company. In this First Folio, the plays were divided into three groups: Comedies, Histories and Tragedies, but a more helpful and significant rearrangement has been as follows: the Early Comedies, the Chronicles, the Histories, the Later Comedies, the Problem Plays, the Roman Plays, the Early Tragedies, the Great Tragedies, the Final Plays.

The time order of these plays has always been a problem and the firm dates of performance or publication will not necessarily provide the exact years in which they were written. The editors of the First Folio in their address made, so prophetically, to the 'great Variety of Readers', warmly describe their old friend's fluency: 'His mind and hand went together: and what he thought he uttered with the easiness that we have scarce received from him a blot in his papers.' This points, therefore, to very careful preparation and knowledge of his topic, since Shakespeare preferred to tell old stories rather than invent new ones, realising that his ability lay in beautifying the ideas of others. His early plays reveal him experimenting with and enjoying his showy, sonneteering style, with plenty of rhymes, but, as he matures and becomes more expert, the poetry is used with restraint and more purpose, to paint character and to deepen emotions.

History was popular, so Shakespeare gave the public the whole, blood-soaked struggle of the English monarchs, from *King John* to the father of Queen Elizabeth, *Henry VIII*. Audiences loved his comedies so he gave them more—the fat knight Sir John Falstaff appeared in *Henry IV* and later in *The Merry Wives of Windsor*, following closely on *Twelfth Night*. The uncertain political situation at the end of the queen's reign made him turn, however, to foreign, ancient history, in the Roman plays and *Troilus and Cressida*. It was safer to show Caesar stabbed by Brutus in the Capitol than *Richard II* deposed by *Henry IV* in England. And anyhow, the public loved the melodrama, blood and thunder, so Mr Shakescene followed the fashion set by the writings of Christopher Marlowe (1564-93) (*Tamburlaine*) and Thomas Kyd (1558?-94?) (*The Spanish Tragedy*) with his own more refined tragedies. We do not know whether the inspiration and motives for writing the tragedies were personal or came from the simple wisdom of following other writers' successes by similar plays with dark revenge themes, but whatever the impulse the results were superb: the four great tragedies: *Hamlet*, *Othello*, *King Lear*, *Macbeth*, then *Antony and Cleopatra* and *Coriolanus*. After the great tragedies the formal convention of the soliloquies gives way to a tighter use of groups of images in the regular dialogue, as in *Antony and Cleopatra*.

The final or romance plays discourse in a more relaxed poetry and a mellower tone, as relief from the black horrors of death, and with repentence and reconciliation after the sin and suffering. Shakespeare was richer in sentimental experience, wealth and years now and so the calmer detachment in the practice of his craft is a natural consequence. But this development may also be partly due to a theatreman's wish to explore the wider opportunities provided for his performers on the roofed, indoor stage at the Blackfriars Theatre from around 1609.

The Blackfriars Theatre marked a new development in the history of the theatre. For their plays the Greeks and Romans had the large open-air theatres, so many of which have survived around the Mediterranean. But in England theatre progressed from the acting of dramatised Bible stories, first inside churches, and then on platforms outside in the open. Morality plays and Interludes, serious and comic, were performed around the country by travelling troupes of actors in tents or inn-yards, halls or fine houses. Then with the Renaissance came Roman plays popularly presented by educated amateurs in schools and by the students of law in the Inns of Court. The need for a permanent operational centre for the drama was first met by the building of The Theatre by James Burbage in 1576. This was the first public playhouse built in England, and it was established only sixteen years before the first mention of Shakespeare occurs—the comment by Greene which alludes to him as an already successful dramatist in London. Roman theatres were round; the Elizabethan structures also followed this shape, roughly, since they had a circular interior pit, open to the sky, surrounded by tiers of seats in three galleries, like those in the inn-yards, but enclosed by an octagonal outer wall. The stage was a large raised platform, thrusting well out into the pit, where the spectators stood for the performance. A roofed canopy, jutting out to cover part of the stage supported on two columns, was known as the Heaven, or Shadow. Behind this was the inner stage, recessed rooms on two levels both of which could be curtained off. Behind this were the dressing and store rooms. Thus a variety of acting areas and levels with doors and steps for access was provided, over which the scenes could be dispersed according to the needs of the play. Costly costumes of the day, with plenty of realistic properties, along with music and sound effects, made it possible to present the intentions of the playwright convincingly, swiftly and excitingly with no scenery or front curtain.

The citizen: 'Sweet Master Shakespeare'

Shakespeare grew up and began working in the last two decades of Queen Elizabeth's reign, a time when a multitude of exciting things was happening all round him; new ideas were being exchanged and new ventures achieved.

He was not only a child but a man of the time, 'possessing' it, sharing it and then helping to make the Elizabethan Age the most significant in the history of England. Being born and brought up in the country and marrying a farmer's daughter he knew 'country matters', was a child also of nature, familiar with biological processes, and also respecting the decreed order of growing things, the inevitable progression of birth, reproduction, and death. From his years in Stratford he knew not only the affairs of marketing produce, crops and animals, but also the trading and commerce of skilled handiwork and manufactures.

In the country, traditions were strong and the people were superstitious, many still believing in witches and fairies. But Stratford was an important enough town to receive visits of the official court companies of players, some of which took place while Shakespeare's father was mayor. The players and their performances were popular since they showed something of the life of the great world outside Warwickshire.

It was to and from London (the capital city of the five million inhabitants of England and Wales, by then containing a hundred thousand citizens), that the restless people and the new ideas moved, within and around the brilliant court where the virgin Queen Elizabeth (1558–1603), known as the Phoenix of the World, ruled, determinedly supreme as mistress over all and wife of none.

As the prospering Shakespeare, performing for the queen, came closer to the seat of power, he appreciated more the enormous problems she and all other monarchs must face and solve, at home and abroad, in order to survive. He learnt that men will protest, fight, and die to keep their beliefs, their persons and their countries free.

This vain but talented and highly educated queen kept the balances cunningly in a struggle of religious and political intrigue, encouraging the sensational ideas of the Renaissance, and helping England to blossom from a medieval society to the most efficient modern state in Europe. Shakespeare realised that it was the courage, vitality and tolerance of men that mattered. The great disputes about gods, the many of the Greeks and the Romans, and the bitterly disputed one of the Christians, Jews and Moslems were acceptable as part of the agreed order of life. But it was natural, spiritual and mortal man, at the centre, the proper secular strong but gentle man, who must keep control of the order, who was the chief, fascinated concern of Shakespeare. The divine order of the Universe was represented in the Great Chain of Being by God, attended by his angels. Then came the planets, the spheres, the stars, which controlled the destinies of Mankind, whose nature was composed of four elements: air, fire, earth and water. Man had at his command the animals, plants and metals. But although the queen was the earthly pivot of this system, she was surrounded by the brightest stars in the realms of the arts and sciences: in drama, poetry, painting, music, architecture, mathematics, astronomy, geography, physics and botany. An increasing number of books were now being published on all branches of science; Galileo was born the same year as Shakespeare, and major advances were being made in astronomy, the study of the worlds in space beyond our own. These helped the great explorers to navigate their better equipped ships to embrace new continents, new worlds eastwards and westwards across the seas, the most important achievement of the age.

The influences coming in from Italy, France, Germany, the Low Countries (Holland) and Spain, and from further distant places overseas, must have been experienced by Shakespeare in conversations as well as in reading. How well he distilled them into the magic of his poetic drama!

Shakespeare and Plutarch

Plutarch's *Parallel Lives of the noble Greeks and Romans* (1579), one of the great books of the world, was used extensively by Shakespeare for his three Roman plays, and, in part, for *Timon of Athens*. It contained biographies and deep character studies of Julius Caesar, Brutus, Cassius, Coriolanus and Mark Antony, in which was the story of the unsociable Timon.

Sir Thomas North's excellent translation from the French made *The Lives* a national classic and it obviously fascinated Shakespeare. He perhaps read it on its first publication, when he was fifteen, or more likely in the 1595 edition, some time before he wrote *Julius Caesar*. Here were the stories of the greatest men of Greece and Rome presented not just as highlights of antiquity but as human beings, who by their special personalities and decisions shaped their times into history.

Plutarch wrote in the first century AD, probably not more than a hundred years after the death of Antony, but soon enough to hear personal experiences from his great-grandfather about the Battle of Actium, and from even his grandfather about Antony's generous entertaining in Alexandria. He was a Greek philosopher, and so his sympathies ran more towards his fellow countrymen than the Roman subjects of his detailed studies. Shakespeare, distilling North's version at the time when his creative skills were at their height, was able to use both the language and the stories exactly to suit his intentions. In many cases he remains remarkably faithful to the original, for example in the famous speech by Enobarbus praising Cleopatra (II.2.193), but he sometimes left out unfavourable comments and expanded the material, adding his own in order to create his plays and to evoke the special atmosphere for his verse translation from the prose of the biographer.

What makes Plutarch's account of Antony and Cleopatra so brightly vivid is his use not only of personal sources, and the writings of Cleopatra's doctor Olympus, but also of his own memories of Egypt, which was the first country he visited on his travels.

Shakespeare smoothly cuts Plutarch's eleven years of Antony's history into a swiftly moving plot, packed with intense sensibility, tailoring the time and personalities of the chief characters, as he relates their love story in this most powerful poetic drama. The poet fills in Antony's generosity and popularity with his men; he cuts out suggestions of Cleopatra's disloyalty, and invents actions by Octavius in order to increase our sympathies for the lovers, and yet, strangely, in his need for speed, he does not mention that Antony stayed four years with his wife, Octavia, before returning to Cleopatra. Furthermore, from a Senator included by Plutarch only twice, Shakespeare creates Enobarbus, a major figure in the play.

Shakespeare, while compressing events, effectively extended their setting in the world, as it was then known from the remarkable map of the ancient geographer Claudius Ptolemy, who studied the stars in Alexandra around AD150. Although the palaces of the queen's capital enclose it, the action moves swiftly round the Mediterranean, through Italy, Sicily and Greece, and into Turkey and Syria (Asia), which is the farthest eastwards of any scene in Shakespeare. This vast scope of action with its feeling of extended space stresses the drama of the trio within it, who are struggling for command of an empire, which for them is the entire civilised world.

A note on the text

The first known, published version of the play appeared in the First Folio in 1623, with thirty-five others, *Pericles* having been omitted. *The Tragedie of Antony and Cleopatra*, as Shakespeare called it, is one of the seventeen plays which were, in this way, printed for the first time, the other eighteen having already been issued, in the smaller quarto-sized editions. It is helpful to have some idea of when the plays were written, and publication dates help scholars to clear up complications of meaning, and to adjust misprints in the text. We should remember that a play is created first to be performed. If it succeeds then it may be published because the audience wish to read the story after having seen it on the stage. Now, Shakespeare wrote his plays, often swiftly, for his team; as that, in addition to acting, was his job, for which he received a special share of the production's profits. The play, however, remained the property of the company. From Shakespeare's own original manuscript other working copies would be made to be used by the director, the prompter (the man who reminds the actors of their entrances and lines), and those responsible for the other stage work, such as music, battle and storm noises.

These few copies of popular plays would be highly valued by the company for repeat performances later, but also by rival companies for their pirated or stolen productions, and lastly by the rich and educated playgoers, increasing in number as Shakespeare's work was appreciated, for inclusion in their libraries as properly printed books.

Shakespeare had taken care to see that his long poems were printed accurately, but for some reason he was unable to ensure the same checking for a number of the plays in the Quarto edition, probably printed without his permission. This resulted in many textural problems, from which, however, *Antony and Cleopatra* is to a great extent free, having fortunately been printed from a good manuscript, probably the poet's own, or from a clean transcription, from which misprints could be easily corrected.

Part 2

Summaries
of ANTONY AND CLEOPATRA

General summary

Mark Antony, Lepidus and Octavius Caesar are the triumvirs, the three-man team, who have divided the Roman world after their victory at Philippi over Cassius and Brutus, the assassins of Julius Caesar. Antony, who is the eastern commander, has become so devoted to Cleopatra, the Queen of Egypt, that he is neglecting his duties and his wife in Rome. When he realises from the rebellion of his wife, Fulvia, and his brother against Caesar, how much danger and resentment his prolonged stay in Alexandria has caused, he decides that he must leave Cleopatra. She strongly resists this, revealing, after he has gone, how deeply she loves him.

In Rome after a cool meeting with Caesar and Lepidus, Antony agrees, in an effort to keep the alliance together, to marry Octavia, Caesar's sister. Sextus, the younger son of Pompey the Great, emboldened by Antony's absence in Egypt, has become so popular and powerful at sea that the reunited triumvirs arrange to meet him at Misenum, north of Rome, 'to talk before they fight'.

Back in Egypt the news brought to the impatient Cleopatra of Antony's remarriage enrages her, and she demands to hear the fullest description of Octavia's attractions which from the frightened messenger's words she is comforted to think are inferior to her own.

In Caesar's house the soothsayer warns Antony that his guardian-angel, though noble, always feels overcome in the presence of Caesar, and so tells him to leave Rome. Antony admits that he must return to Egypt because, although he has made the marriage for his peace, his pleasure lies back in the East with Cleopatra.

After the banquet given on board Pompey's ship to celebrate their treaty, while Lepidus is carried off drunk, Caesar coolly retires early, leaving Antony and Pompey, now reconciled, to finish their drinking ashore.

However, not long after Antony has gone eastwards to Athens with Octavia, news comes that Caesar has broken the treaty and has first used Lepidus to help him to defeat Pompey, then treacherously imprisoned him. So Antony understands that the world is now divided between him and Caesar, who is becoming so powerful that Octavia goes to Rome to make peace between them, while he speeds back to

Cleopatra. To convince the queen of his good faith he bestows upon her and her children the eastern kingdoms of the Roman empire, in an elaborate public ceremony.

For Caesar, this, with the unannounced arrival in Rome of Octavia, is the final outrage, and although he agrees to give Antony half his new acquisitions he demands the same in return, knowing that this will never be granted, and that war must inevitably follow.

This begins at Actium in northern Greece, where Caesar is victorious, because Antony, against all the warnings of Enobarbus and his generals, agrees with Cleopatra to fight at sea, and then, when she flees during the battle, follows her to Egypt.

This is the beginning of the end for the lovers. Antony is disgusted with himself and with the queen, and is so unable to bear the thought of defeat by the young, despised Caesar that he contemplates suicide. Yet her apologies and his restraint bring about reconciliation, and to Caesar, arriving in Egypt with his army, he sends for peace terms.

Caesar, however, replies that he will listen only to the queen, if she will send Antony away or kill him. This stings Antony into challenging him to fight alone. Disregarding this challenge Caesar sends Thidias with instructions to win Cleopatra from Antony, because he wants her for his triumph in Rome.

Antony, feeling authority melting from him, suspects Cleopatra of flirting, and perhaps betraying him, so has Thidias flogged, while fiercely attacking the queen for her behaviour. Accepting her passionate excuses he again relents and decides that he will fight Caesar, who has now reached the gates of Alexandria. Enobarbus, who has made up his mind to desert, is distressed, as is the queen, when Antony in thanking his servants for their devotion asks for their best service at the feast they are preparing, as though it will be his last. And, indeed, the soldiers on night-watch at the palace, hearing a strange music 'under the earth', take it as a bad omen that 'the God, whom Antony loved' is now abandoning him.

The next day Cleopatra lovingly helps Eros to arm Antony, who hearing, just before the battle, that Enobarbus has gone over to Caesar, sends all his treasure after him. Antony wins the first round and returns overjoyed for what, now, will really be his last night's celebration with Cleopatra. In Caesar's camp Enobarbus, ashamed of his treachery, dies with Antony's name on his lips.

The following morning, on seeing the queen's navy surrendering to the enemy, Antony turns upon her so furiously, intent on killing her, that she takes refuge with her ladies in her unfinished tomb, and sends him a message that she has killed herself. On being told this, Antony, who is already in a suicidal mood himself, immediately commands Eros to kill him. Eros stabs himself instead, and Antony falls on his own sword. But, humiliated by finding that he is only wounded, and that no one else will finish him off, he asks Diomedes to take him, uncomplaining, to the still living Cleopatra.

The dying hero is hoisted in through the window, and after a final cup of wine and kisses, he welcomes death, in the queen's arms. Desolate, she resolves to follow him. Caesar, on news of Antony's death, speaks highly of him but sends Proculeius to encourage Cleopatra not to kill herself.

This he does, having by trickery entered the 'monument' and captured the queen. Caesar then visits her but she, mistrustful, outwits him and goes ahead with her preparations to join Antony.

Dressed once more in all her regalia she takes the snake from a basket of figs, brought to her, as planned, by a countryman, and dies of poison. Caesar accepts his defeat by the lovers, and orders that Cleopatra shall be buried with Antony, with all the solemnity of a state funeral.

Detailed summaries

Act I Scene 1

In the royal palace in Alexandria two Roman officers, Philo and Demetrius, complain of the bad effect which the obsession of their general Antony for the queen has had upon him. This seems to be confirmed when Cleopatra enters, with Antony, demanding to be told how much he really loves her. His efforts to explain this prevent him from receiving the messengers from Rome. Cleopatra mocks him, saying that perhaps he should listen to what may well be commands to return from either his wife Fulvia or his young colleague Octavius Caesar. He protests angrily that he does not care about Rome and the Empire, but to stay there in Egypt loving her is the noblest thing he can do. He asks her, therefore, to stop arguing and to start their night's pleasures with a walk through the streets to see how the ordinary people live.

NOTES AND GLOSSARY:
This is a brilliant introduction, giving us in miniature, in only sixty-two lines, a vivid preview of the great couple and their struggles. Twice Shakespeare effectively uses the dramatic trick of bringing on characters, first Philo and then Cleopatra, in the middle of conversations. Cleopatra's domination of Antony, at first, and then her needling of him, show us her fear of losing him to Rome, and provoke him to the thunderous and shocking denial of his ambitions and obligations. Nevertheless, Shakespeare clearly suggests the genuineness and nobility of their love, in Antony's last two speeches. It will be the differences

between Egypt and Rome and their understandings of love that will cause the tragedy.

dotage:	infatuation
files and musters:	ranks of troops
tawny:	light brown
reneges:	renounces
strumpet:	prostitute
bourn:	limit
enfranchise:	liberate
homager:	servant
twain:	couple
wrangling:	argumentative
chide:	reprove

Act I Scene 2

The soothsayer tells the fortunes of the ladies-in-waiting. Cleopatra comes in briefly but avoids meeting Antony, who follows and now hears the messengers from Rome, whose news is that Fulvia has first fought against his brother Lucius, and then, both together, they have battled against Caesar, and been defeated. He also hears that the Parthians have successfully advanced from Syria to the shores of Asia (Turkey). The second messenger tells him that Fulvia has died in Greece, on her way to meet him. Antony, realising at last that his neglect has created this serious situation, tells Enobarbus of his decision to return to Rome. Enobarbus coarsely foretells that this will cause trouble with Cleopatra, whom he praises, while speaking lightly of Fulvia's death. But Antony rebukes him, adding the increasing power of Pompey as another urgent reason for their return, orders for which are then given.

NOTES AND GLOSSARY:

Except for the speeches of Antony this scene is in prose, more suitable to the changes of mood and the free sexuality of the subordinates' talk. It is an interlude to emphasise the warm sensuality of the Egyptian court in contrast to the cool, harsh and urgent formality of Rome, which we now see Antony assuming in his speech as he takes on 'a Roman thought' (1.75).

The words of the fortune-teller spark off the salty jokes of Charmian and Iras but also foretell their fates. A further flash forward is given in Charmian's indelicate but ironic words '. . . I love long life better than figs' (1.30), which will later come into our minds when she dies by the same poison as that which Cleopatra takes from the basket of figs. Compare the warnings of the soothsayer in the later scene (II.3.19). Enobarbus is first introduced with few but significant words, calling for food and wine, leading on to his cynical exchanges with Antony over Fulvia and Cleopatra. The characters of both the queen and Antony are subtly deepened so that we can share sympathetically the drama of their parting in the next scene.

garlands: wreaths
prescience: foresight
presageth: foretells
cuckold: man whose wife is unfaithful
rail: reproach
alack: alas
almanacs: books forecasting events, published yearly
smock: a loose dress
abode: dwelling-place

Act I Scene 3

Seven times Antony tries to tell Cleopatra of his departure but is interrupted by the moody queen. He is purposeful, so she is weak, pretending to faint; he is tender, she asks him to move away; he is puzzled, and she mocks him, attacking him for his infidelity to both Fulvia and herself, until at last he is allowed to give her a concentrated account of his true and urgent reasons for leaving. But the last of these, Fulvia's death, which should be the strongest reassurance for her, sets off a fresh outburst and her final triple insult that he, a Roman, descended from the god Hercules, is only acting his grief. When she sees that she has gone too far she instantly changes, accepting that 'honour calls' him, then asking to be forgiven she wishes him 'smooth success'.

NOTES AND GLOSSARY:
Shakespeare's maturity of both experience and writing is revealed here in the queen's wide range of acting, of which she ironically accuses Antony. This is another scene which builds up character, shocking us at first with Cleopatra's tricks while we admire Antony's patient control. Therefore, as their actions reveal their deep love for each other, so their language adds impressive inches to their stature. Cleopatra's speech, 'Pray you seek no colour', and Antony's explanatory reply, 'The strong necessity of time', in particular reveal this. Before their separation the poet has thus clearly shown the highly emotional relationship between the royal Egyptian mistress and her enchanted Roman general.

forbear: abstain, withdraw
bent: curve
faction: party struggles
apace: quickly
garboils: commotions, troubles

vials:	small bottles
quickens:	brings alive
dissembling:	pretence
target:	shield
chafe:	anger
becomings:	feelings, behaviour

Act I Scene 4

Caesar and Lepidus in Rome are discussing Antony's soft, loose life in Alexandria, before they learn of the rising strength of Pompey and the pirates Menas and Menecrates, who threaten the coasts of Italy. Lepidus is more tolerant of Antony, while Caesar, recalling his past courage and stamina as a campaigning general, invokes him to leave his lustful revelry and come to their assistance.

NOTES AND GLOSSARY:
There are no couches, fans or wine shown here in Rome, but letters and politics instead of love. Here are Antony's two 'competitors' who swiftly reveal their characters in their reactions to the news of his conduct. This is the Octavius whose ruthlessness made him the first Roman emperor, arrogantly referring to himself as 'Caesar' in the third person, or 'we' in the royal plural, talking down from these august heights to the kindlier and so weaker Lepidus. Caesar as public prosecutor is here stating the case against Antony, with tight-lipped distaste of his goings-on in Egypt. But we should notice two things: it is not the actions themselves which anger Caesar, who becomes almost human in the telling of them, but their result, the loss to him of Antony's power, which he resents. Contrast the style of his second, Alexandria speech (1.16) with his third about Pompey and popularity (1.40), and the difference in the two contemptuous descriptions of the mob: 'knaves that smell of sweat' (1.21) and 'this common body' (1.44). But Shakespeare must strengthen Antony's character and so cleverly makes Caesar remember the rigorous Modena campaign (ll.57-71), borne bravely by Antony, 'so like a soldier', which is the quality he needs so urgently against Pompey.

vouchsafed:	deigned, accepted
enow:	enough
reel:	stagger along
foils:	shameful actions
surfeits:	excesses
ebbed:	in the lowest state
wassails:	drinking sessions
lascivious:	indecent
stale:	urine

gilded:	covered with yellow scum
deign:	accept
browsed:	fed upon
lanked:	grew thin
stirs:	events
mandragora:	mandrake plant juice

Act I Scene 5

Cleopatra, anxious, trying to 'sleep out the great gap of time', while her Antony is away, wonders what he is doing and thinking in Rome. When asking him, the 'demi-Atlas of this earth', to think of her sunburnt and ageless, the passage of time reminds her of the two other great men who had loved her: Julius Caesar and Gnaeus Pompey, the elder brother of Sextus. But she loves Antony so much that she sends messengers to him every day; twenty of them were met by Alexas, who now brings the longed-for news, with a pearl, as a symbol of his constant love, and the promise of all the kingdoms of the East. Could she have loved Julius Caesar as much, she enquires of Charmian, whom she then threatens to hit, if she praises Caesar more. No, in those days she was green in judgement, now Antony is her 'man of men'.

NOTES AND GLOSSARY:
Here Shakespeare pauses to deepen the colours of his portrait of the queen, with her behaviour, desires and recollections, and the vividness of her language. We are shown both aspects of the coin of their love, which by its intensity, and the genuine affection of both sides, is made to ring true. The lover who stays waiting is always the greater sufferer, and Cleopatra, here in the warm comfort of her court, misses her man, 'that great med'cine' (1.36), so in fantasy she speculates ('delicious poison' (1.27)) not only about Antony's appearance and actions but also on his thoughts about herself. Characteristically the want of his physical attentions drives her to unkind innuendo with the eunuch (ll.9–10), unreasonable threats against Charmian (1.70) for her unwise praise of Julius Caesar, and against the people of Egypt (1.78) to provide enough postmen for her daily delivery. These prepare us for her savage treatment of the messenger later (II.5). The metaphors are rich and loaded with sexual implication: deed (1.15); O happy horse (1.21); serpent (1.25); Phoebus' amorous pinches (1.28); morsel (1.31); salad days (1.73). Antony's gift of the much-kissed pearl, rare from the Orient, is his clear promise, as the 'firm Roman' not only of Eastern kingdoms but the proof of fidelity, his intention to return to protect the throne from which she may securely rule them.

bond:	duty

unseminared:	seedless
wot:	know
burgonet:	light helmet
morsel:	piece of food
gilded:	made golden
arm-gaunt:	worn thin (meaning uncertain)
paragon:	compare
salad:	young, inexperienced

Act II Scene 1

In Sicily, we have our first sight of Sextus Pompey with his fellow pirates. He is the confident man of the moment and the threat to the triumvirate, but happy only when believing that Antony will not leave Egypt. He calls upon Cleopatra to ensure this by using all her spells and charms. But Varrius brings the grave news that Antony has, after all, left for Rome. Pompey, knowing that the great soldier is worth 'twice the other twain', is flattered that it is fear of him which has torn Antony from 'the lap of Egypt's widow'. But he realises that the triumvirs will now have to patch up their quarrels to unite against him.

NOTES AND GLOSSARY:
This is the younger son of Pompey the Great, who, set on avenging the defeat of his father by Caesar, is now challenging his adopted son and heir, our Octavius Caesar. With Pompey's self-revealing account of his power and shrewd evaluation of his opponents' weaknesses we get another view of the Antony and Cleopatra affair. He is powerful at sea, is winning those hearts which Caesar loses by taxation, and scornfully thinks that because Antony 'In Egypt sits at dinner', that he will not fight abroad. The insincerity of Lepidus is shared by all, and, so Pompey believes, is no danger. Just as Caesar called upon Antony before, now Pompey with rolling phrases ringing with the delights of bed and banquet implores Cleopatra to hold Antony in Egypt. The force of this wish increases the dramatic shock of the instant news that Antony and all his soldierly strength are now in Rome. Pompey's forecast that the disagreements there will be mended is confirmed in the next scene.

crescent:	growing
auguring:	foretelling
libertine:	man given to immoral pleasures
epicurean:	who caters for pleasure-lovers
cloyless:	unable to satisfy
Lethe:	underworld river causing forgetfulness
helm:	helmet
pregnant:	obvious, clear

Act II Scene 2

Neutral Lepidus is host in Rome for the meeting with his two great colleagues, and he asks Enobarbus to restrain Antony, if necessary, but this Enobarbus refuses to do. Antony and Caesar enter at the same time, symbolically from opposite sides. They will not even greet each other until Lepidus begs them to debate without anger. Antony immediately denies responsibility for Fulvia's wars, admitting that she acted to get him away from Egypt. He claimed that he had a hangover when the messengers broke in unannounced, and that his gay life in Egypt had made him neglect, not refuse, to send aid to Caesar. Antony's confessions and apologies satisfy Lepidus and Maecenas, but Enobarbus's comment that they all might, at least, pretend to be friends until Pompey's threat was past, irritates both Antony and Caesar, who doubts if they can ever agree, having such opposed characters. Agrippa rescues them from this deadlock by proposing that Antony, now a widower, can marry Caesar's sister Octavia, to which they both agree with relief. Antony then announces that before they fight he wishes to thank Pompey for his recent kindnesses to him, and it is agreed that they must confront him in Misenum, after the wedding, which they now go to discuss with Octavia.

As a change from the hard business of Rome Maecenas and Agrippa question Enobarbus concerning life in Egypt, the pleasures of which he is glad to describe, and in particular the wonders of Cleopatra, and her enchantment of Antony, when she sailed majestically to meet him in Tarsus.

NOTES AND GLOSSARY:
This is the most subtly intense scene in the first half of the play, being the direct confrontation of the two men, who will as a result of it have to fight each other for the world: Antony for love and honour, Caesar for naked power. We know their qualities and now see them in single, verbal combat. The stalemate is temporarily resolved by the sacrifice of Caesar's sister, the innocent Octavia, upon the altar of their urgent need for peace.

Each reader will have to make up his own mind on this much discussed question: did either of them really believe, or even hope, that the marriage would last? Only careful study of every word and their delicate shades of meaning in this and the next scene can help us to decide what Shakespeare intended. He shows his skill by changing history to suit his situations, in this case telescoping time, because Antony remained with Octavia for four years. But he makes this desertion acceptable by providing some compensatory causes for it: the Cydnus speech, the soothsayer, Octavia's unexciting, though noble, qualities, and Caesar's actions. Those who have read *Julius Caesar* (IV.3) will realise that in Antony's forceful opening remarks there is a reminder of the more familiar quarrel scene between Brutus and Cassius, and there are also echoes of this at two peak moments when Caesar's accusations are so strong that we expect an outburst from Antony. The first, the suggestion that Antony was plotting against him from Egypt, is so shocking (ll.43-4) that Antony asks him to explain himself. At the second, 'you have broken the article of your faith', even Lepidus warns Caesar to be careful (l.87).

Having defended his charges with open, informal excuses in contrast to Caesar's clipped, biting words, joking about the domineering Fulvia, and admitting his drinking in Alexandria, Antony, with a smile to Caesar, has kept his temper well throughout, since he apologises gracefully, mentioning honour again. The frankness with which he confesses his 'poisoned hours' (l.94) and the real cause of Fulvia's wars, wins over all except Caesar, until Agrippa's marriage proposal.

Pompey's 'strange courtesies' (l.159) were his kind reception of Antony's mother and Fulvia after her defeat by Caesar when they fled from Italy. After the strain of these cheerless politics Caesar's ministers are given Enobarbus's account of the gossip and gay life in the palace at Alexandria, and specially about the queen, always an object of Eastern mystery to the Romans.

The placing here, immediately after Antony's agreement to wed Octavia, of this colourful description (ll.194-229) of his meeting with Cleopatra, spoken in such superb poetry by the usually blunt soldier Enobarbus, is masterly. And then, after his first-hand assessment of the woman herself, the suggestion by Maecenas that Octavia's beauty, wisdom and modesty 'will settle the heart of Antony' can only sound hopelessly optimistic.

curstness:	bad temper
snaffle:	bridle, bit for a horse
gibe:	laugh, joke
ruminated:	considered, thought about
square:	true, faithful
burnished:	polished
poop:	ship's high stern
pavilion:	large tent, awning
Nereides:	sea nymphs
tackle:	ropes of a boat
yarely:	quickly
ordinary:	public meal
cropped:	bore a child (Caesarion)
cloy:	fill to disgust
riggish:	lustful, wanton

Act II Scene 3

Our first glimpse of gentle Octavia in Caesar's house must compete with Cleopatra's ageless and 'infinite variety', so vividly described before. In Caesar's presence Antony asks for Octavia's understanding, during his absences, in spite of his bad reputation, because he promises good behaviour from now on. They say goodnight and in comes the soothsayer, who urges Antony to return to Egypt quickly, because he sees Caesar's fortunes turning on the wheel will rise higher than his. Antony's guardian spirit is brave and unbeatable until confronted by 'shining' Caesar. Antony dismisses him but confirms that the ominous words are true, and they provide another excuse, so soon after the marriage, for his return to Egypt, while Ventidius will be sent to fight the Parthians.

NOTES AND GLOSSARY:
Octavia shows cool modesty and humility in the only two sentences she is given to speak. The soothsayer, who has reluctantly come from Egypt, reveals the spiritual domination over Antony of Caesar's demon when they are together. This has been evident so far only in the speed with which Antony agreed to the marriage. But he confirms his unease, having had ten years to be made aware of it, and there is surely an element of relief in his 'pleasure' to get away to the East (l.39).

Ventidius, seen with Antony in II.2.15, is now given his orders for Parthia, to prepare us for his appearance in Syria describing his victories (III.1) on Antony's behalf.

office:	duties
sirrah:	you (to an inferior)
lustre:	brilliance
quails:	small birds

Act II Scene 4

A linking scene out of doors, so brief that the words between Lepidus and Caesar's chief generals can be exchanged while walking down a Roman street. They discuss the speed (Antony will only have time to kiss Octavia) with which, by different routes, they will reach Misenum to fight Pompey. Lepidus with his greater responsibilities will take longer.

NOTES AND GLOSSARY:
| **conceive:** | plan |
| **Mount:** | Mount Mesena |

Act II Scene 5

To give time for the journey to Misenum we are now shown the queen, still waiting in Alexandria and unable to settle to any one pastime. Fishing reminds Charmian and Cleopatra of past tricks and amorous games she played with Antony, and leads to the entrance of the messenger, bringing news of Octavia's wedding, which he tries eight times to announce. Unbelieving and furious, the queen knocks him down, pulls his hair and, when he finally confirms the news, tries to stab him, at which he runs out. Twice more after his reluctant return he is made to confirm the marriage. He complains that it is unfair to punish him for telling the truth, which she accepts, yet dismisses him with a curse. Now, she admits, Caesar has got the better of her for her love of Antony, whom she never wishes to see again. Even so, she sends Alexas to report back to her on Octavia's attractions.

NOTES AND GLOSSARY:
There is so little action while Antony is away that words must speak vividly in Cleopatra's image-packed speeches. We expect trouble from the moment the messenger enters, and until the words are out (l.60): 'Madam, he's married to Octavia', the suspense is tensely built up. The queen's violence is shocking proof of her love, which compels her to behave so unmajestically but humanly. From this we get a further idea of the passionate temperament which Antony has to put up with but still adores.

billiards:	game
angle:	fishing-rod
Philippan:	from the battle of Philippi
formal:	ordinary, conventional
allay:	take away from
spurn:	kick
pickle:	preserving liquid
cistern:	tank, pond
Gorgon:	Medusa, snake-haired monstress

Act II Scene 6

Pompey in Misenum explains that he is confronting the allies because they destroyed Cassius and Brutus, who died fighting for the same republican ideals as his father did, by opposing the ambitious Julius Caesar.

But realising that, in spite of his supremacy at sea, he is not strong enough to win now that Antony is with them, he accepts their terms. He had, however, almost refused them because of Antony's apparently ungrateful attitude. For this Antony gives the thanks and apologies which he had prepared, and Pompey accepts them, admitting that he had not expected him to leave Egypt. Antony turns this insinuation by thanking him for forcing him to come, and for the advantages he has thus gained. Caesar comments on the change he sees in Pompey, who asks for the treaty to be officially sealed before they all feast each other. Yet he cannot resist taunting Antony and begins to tell the story of how Cleopatra was brought first to Julius Caesar, but is stopped by Enobarbus, whose plain speaking he respects. Once again Enobarbus stays behind, now in conversation with Menas, to emphasise the frailty of Antony's marriage. Menas, who is not happy about the treaty, asks him aboard the galley.

NOTES AND GLOSSARY:
Under the formal, negotiating exteriors of these Romans we are shown the fear, mistrust, resentment and human interests that motivate their intrigues for security and power. Caesar, as usual, is terse and aggressive, Pompey is nervous and particularly irritated with Antony, who is ill at ease under his obligations to him, but takes calmly the untimely insinuations about Cleopatra (ll.63 and 68). Enobarbus extends his frankness to both Pompey and Menas, with whom his swift exchanges give a summary of the various situations up to the moment: the treaty, the feasts, Cleopatra, Octavia's wedding, and the slim chances, as a result, of the survival of the alliance.

Act II Scene 7

Music and some critical comments by the servants introduce us to the banquet on board Pompey's ship. While Antony makes fun of Lepidus with his crocodiles, Menas offers to slit the throats of the triumvirs. Pompey coolly says that he should have done this without telling him, but that he cannot condone it. This decides Menas to desert him for missing such an opportunity. These double standards are stressed as Enobarbus points at Lepidus being carried off drunk. Caesar protests at the effect of the wine, by replying ominously to Antony's warm 'Be a child o' the time', that is 'relax and enjoy yourself', with 'Possess it', meaning 'No, be master of the moment'. After Enobarbus leads them in the drunken dance, Caesar has had enough, and as they go ashore Pompey forgives Antony for taking over his father's house in Rome and declares friendship.

NOTES AND GLOSSARY:
After the formality of the conference scenes the humour, free action and unusual setting of this vivid interlude are welcome. But although the

liberal drinking makes for comedy, nevertheless, it contributes to an atmosphere of uncertainty and menace beneath the surface. It is a tightly constructed exercise in aspects of human nature, illustrating in three movements that things are seldom what they seem. Antony's clear and accurate exposition of the Nile flooding is followed by his deliberate fooling of the fuddled Lepidus in his mock-serious description of the crocodile. This is calculated fun, but chilled by Menas's naked suggestion of mass murder and Pompey's unashamedly cynical refusal of it. Then, as one of the 'rulers of the world' is hauled off, dead drunk, the others stagger round the deck, singing to Bacchus. Antony, more in his element here, dominates the show, which makes the point of how hypocritical it is for the Romans, when they behave like this, to condemn Antony in Egypt, since his life there is for a single, honest motive—Cleopatra.

factors:	agents
rig:	fit out for sea
targes:	targets, shields
vassal:	servant
alms-drink:	dregs
foison:	plenty, abundance
dearth:	famine, little
pyramises:	pyramids
inclips:	embraces, encloses
bachanals:	ceremonies for Bacchus
plumpy:	fat
fats:	vats, wine
anticked:	made foolish

Act III Scene 1

Antony's general, Ventidius, in Syria, has now avenged the treacherous murder of the Consul Crassus in 53BC by the Parthian king Orodes, whose son Pacorus he has killed in battle. But when Silius suggests that if they follow up this victory they can push the Parthians right back into Persia itself, and thus gain honours from Antony, Ventidius explains why it is not wise to do so. It is risky, he sadly confesses, to do better than one's general, because he will become envious and promotion will be threatened. So he will write to Antony, describing how, in his name, they have now beaten the hitherto invincible Parthian cavalry, and then go to join him in Athens.

NOTES AND GLOSSARY:
While the rulers of the empire drink themselves silly with Pompey, their general Ventidius wins a most important victory far away in the

East. This not only extends frontiers but goes to wipe out the disgrace of the former defeat of Crassus. Envy, another unpleasant side of human nature, is emphasised here by Shakespeare in Ventidius's explanation of his refusal to chase the Parthians further, because, he says, this success would make the absent Antony jealous. His bitter but honest comment that both Caesar and Antony, while absent themselves, have always achieved success through their generals, reminds us of Antony's complaint of Caesar's inactivity at Philippi later (III.11.35), and Antony's own disastrous campaign against the Parthians, which is only mentioned at his attempted suicide, by Eros (IV.14.69). This is the furthest east of all the scenes in Shakespeare's plays, and helps to give a brief rest to the main characters. The lack of loyalty and trust, expressed so clearly here, will come to be the main cause of the disaster that follows, between masters and men on both sides, and also between Antony, Caesar and Cleopatra.

darting:	swift-riding, arrow-shooting
jaded:	driven like tired horses
purposeth:	intends to go

Act III Scene 2

Back in Rome, we hear Enobarbus advancing the story to Agrippa, following the banquet. Pompey, satisfied, has gone away, and while sad Caesar, sick Lepidus and Antony seal their treaty, Octavia weeps to be leaving her brother. They make fun of how 'noble' Lepidus flatters their two commanders, joking as to whom he professes to love best: Caesar, the 'Jupiter of Men', or Antony, 'thou Arabian bird'. This builds up their entrance for the leave-taking. Caesar warns his new brother-in-law threateningly to treat Octavia well, and this almost provokes him. Their farewell makes both Octavia and Caesar weep, which doubting Enobarbus considers unmanly, but reminds Agrippa that Antony wept at the deaths of both Julius Caesar and Brutus. Caesar promises to write, and Antony pretends to wrestle (for their love) as he gives him a final brotherly hug.

NOTES AND GLOSSARY:
The keen observations of Enobarbus once more push the story forward, away from Rome (where there will be only one more scene, the direct result of this one, when Octavia returns to plead for peace with Caesar). This is the last time in the play that Caesar will see Antony alive. The sadness of Caesar's parting from his sister is accentuated by his threat and (remember the soothsayer) Antony's instant and suspicious reaction to it, also their strong mutual affection and the secret which they share. Caesar clearly dominates her, but is slightly humanised by his

weeping. Antony's sudden flash of poetry at Octavia's tears:

> The April's in her eyes; it is love's spring,
> And these the showers to bring it on. Be cheerful. (ll.43–4)

are delicate, high relief.

Enobarbus indicates further cynicism about Antony's wet eyes, saying that he had a cold at Philippi, and Antony's little farewell scuffle with Caesar, perhaps a symbolic contest over their love for Octavia, reminds us that he will twice challenge him to fight in single combat after Actium. We are made to feel that Antony will dutifully try his best to love Octavia, as we know he did, in fact.

dispatched:	arranged matters
green-sickness:	anaemic love-sickness
nonpareil:	unequalled
Arabian bird:	Phoenix
shards:	wings
rheum:	cold, watering of eyes

Act III Scene 3

Now we flash to Egypt for contrast, to Cleopatra and Octavia. The messenger, again understandably frightened, describes Octavia as he believes the queen will wish to see her: short, awkward, round-faced, with brown hair above a low forehead. His tact pleases Cleopatra so that she apologises for her earlier treatment and rewards him.

NOTES AND GLOSSARY:
Cleopatra's changeable character and determination shine through this amusing scene. She must know what she has to fear in her rival, although she is quite aware that she is being flattered by the terrified envoy, and so is ashamed of her former harsh behaviour towards him.

There are two reminders that Antony has left her: when she asks how she can have Herod's head without Antony, now, to command it (l.5), and a vivid link with the preceding scene from the messenger's firm statement:

> I looked her in the face, and saw her led
> Between her brother and Mark Antony. (l.9)

dread:	feared
gait:	way of walking
prithee:	pray thee

Act III Scene 4

Nearer to Egypt now, as the clouds darken, Antony complains in Athens to Octavia of Caesar's actions against him in Rome. She begs him not to believe nor resent what he hears. How can she pray properly for both her husband and her brother to win, when wars between them would be so disastrous?

Antony therefore grants her request to return to Rome to act as a go-between, but warns her that meanwhile he must prepare a greater army than Caesar's, and that eventually she will have to choose which of them more deserves her entire support and love.

NOTES AND GLOSSARY:

Antony enters, vigorously replying to words of Octavia spoken before, but which we soon understand were to excuse her brother's actions to him. We shall recall that Caesar had accused Antony of breaking his promise, but this attack of his on Pompey is a far more serious breach of faith, since all three triumvirs signed the treaty. Caesar's bid for popularity by leaving money to the people in his will, which he read aloud, will remind those who have read *Julius Caesar* of the other will, of the other Caesar, which, read out by Antony, helped to turn the people against the conspirators. The world is now starting to crack, and although historically there were at least two peace attempts by Octavia we feel from Antony's last speech that he must get back to Egypt, where his destiny lies, while Octavia will be safer in Rome.

semblable: similar, seeming like
scantly: grudgingly
presently: now, at once
branchless: without honour
solder up: cement together
rift: break, split
cleave: split:

Act III Scene 5

Elsewhere in the same house Enobarbus and Eros, Antony's freedman, discuss the news that Pompey has been attacked by Caesar with the help of Lepidus, and later executed. Then they tell how Caesar has imprisoned Lepidus on a charge of treachery. Thus, Enobarbus comments, the world is now left to be fought for by Caesar and Antony, who is furious that one of his officers was used to murder Pompey.

NOTES AND GLOSSARY:

Antony's men are putting their own interpretation on the news. A similar picture of the two halves of the world divided by the dead is offered, only here it is more horrific: a pair of jaws chewing up the corpses, if Antony and Caesar fight. The navy is ready and Eros expects an immediate attack on Caesar, but Enobarbus suspects the truth, that Antony is for Egypt, and the scene increases our support for him, at this time.

chaps: jaws

Act III Scene 6

Caesar in Rome indignantly describes the presentation by Antony in exotic public ceremony of the eastern kingdoms of the Roman world to Cleopatra and her children.

He also repeats Antony's accusations of his treatment of Pompey and Lepidus, and of new gains unshared, which have all been answered by messengers.

Octavia now arrives unannounced, without the ceremony with which he should, appropriately, have welcomed her, and so, he suggests, like a 'castaway'. Dramatically, he follows up his accusation that Antony has sent her to plead because it is her presence only that has held him from Cleopatra, by saying that he is now, in fact, with Cleopatra, and preparing for war. He tries to comfort her by blaming Antony and necessity for her sad situation, which the gods have made him their agent to avenge.

NOTES AND GLOSSARY:

Although Shakespeare has been steadily building up Antony's justification for returning to Cleopatra he resists the temptation to make a grand scene out of the reconciliation. In fact we hear the news from Caesar's self-righteous lips, when describing the famous 'Donations' scene in the stadium in Alexandria. Caesar's grounds for complaint are: (1) in great public ceremony Antony gave Roman kingdoms to Caesarion (son of Julius Caesar), and Cleopatra's other children by himself, and (2) Cleopatra, gave audiences dressed as the Goddess Isis, and did so at other times.

Octavius was Julius Caesar's adopted son, Caesarion was his natural son by Cleopatra, and so the official recognition of this was a valid threat to Octavius. We then hear from Caesar, again, Antony's charges against him: (1) he did not give him part of Pompey's Sicily, (2) he did not return the ships Antony lent him, (3) he had imprisoned Lepidus, and (4) he had not passed on Antony's share of the revenue.

With Octavia's return we again have the Roman view, condemning Antony's adultery with the Eastern whore, but we are sceptical of this false morality, having been shown the sincerity of their love.

contemning:	despising
stablishment:	possession
habiliments:	dress, clothing
rated:	given
castaway:	someone discarded
abstract:	obstruction
trull:	prostitute

Act III Scenes 7, 8, 9 and 10

Suddenly we are at Actium. Cleopatra is insisting to Enobarbus upon her presence in Antony's camp as the ruler of Egypt, like a man, however distracting her person may be to him, and whatever they may be saying in Rome. Caesar's swift landing on the same coast surprises them all, for which the queen rebukes Antony's negligence. She then supports his decision to fight by sea. Canidius, the general, complains ominously that they are all being led, now, by a woman.

Two short scenes (8 and 9) of ten lines only, show first Caesar and then Antony disposing their armies for battle. Caesar insists that his general, Taurus, does not fight 'till we have done at sea'. The two armies then march symbolically across the stage, and the sounds of naval battle are heard behind. Then Enobarbus comes, horrified, from watching, followed by Scarus, cursing Cleopatra for her flight and for dragging Antony after her, from the still undecided fight. Thus have they, he cries, 'kissed away kingdoms'. Canidius enters to protest that, following Antony's example, he will surrender his army as six kings have already done. But Enobarbus, against his reason, will still stay with Antony's 'wounded chance'.

NOTES AND GLOSSARY:
Actium is on the west coast of Greece, in Epirus, and we are surprised to see Cleopatra here in the camp. Enobarbus in his attempts to persuade her to leave the fighting to Antony tells her the criticism from Rome (thus linking us to the previous scene), which provokes a typical explosive curse from the furious queen: 'Sink Rome, and their tongues rot' (l.15) and which recalls for us Antony's earlier 'Let Rome in Tiber melt' (I.1.33).

But the atmosphere is depressing: Caesar's rapid advance to the coast (l.22); Cleopatra's criticism of Antony for this (l.24); Antony's obstinate insistence on fighting by sea (l.40), after the queen's support for this, against the advice of all others, including the old soldier (l.61): and finally Canidius's agreement with Rome's insult that they are all, now, 'women's men' (l.70). All this suggests disaster. The speed of the next two brief scenes tightens up the excitement that leads us to the naval battle, which has been called a world-shaking event. The language of the shocked onlookers magically springs to life again, properly to describe apparently ignoble actions of both principals, making us share painfully their anger, shame and despair. The three speeches from Scarus (ll.6, 9, 17) are packed with vivid metaphors: 'nag of Egypt', 'like a cow in June', 'vantage like a pair of twins', 'the noble ruin of her magic', 'Claps on his sea-wing', 'like a doting mallard', and they bombard our senses with an overpowering linguistic force.

forespoke:	spoken against
traduced:	criticised
becomed:	suited
impress:	conscription
yare:	swift, quick, nimble
overplus:	extra
descried:	seen, sighted
power:	army, forces
Thetis:	sea-nymph
prescript:	orders
jump:	action
synod:	assembly
cantle:	segment, part
ribaudred:	wanton
loofed:	aloof, at a distance

Act III Scene 11

Antony, back in Alexandria, emerging from a state of shock, realises the full shame of his action, which the very ground proclaims. To his followers he presents his treasure ship, urging them, in vain, to flee to his friends abroad who will help them. He needs them no longer, having decided on a private solution—suicide. Cleopatra, terrified and contrite at his distress and her guilt, tries to approach him, with the help of Eros. At last his attention is attracted and in a surprisingly gentle but utterly dejected tone he accepts her apologies. But twice he reproves her for not understanding how completely in her power his passion has placed him. Now he, once the master of half the world, must humbly beg for terms from Caesar, to whom he has already sent the tutor of their children. But he suddenly submits to her repeated calls for pardon; he begs her not to cry but instead to give him a kiss, which, he says with splendid generosity, 'alone repays me'. He now regains his determination to defy fortune.

NOTES AND GLOSSARY:
So persuasive is Shakespeare that we accept this confrontation as

though it were their first after the flight from Actium. Antony is like a great wounded bull in the ring, but his language in adversity is rich and warm to his friends. His care about them and forgiveness of Cleopatra build up our sympathy, countering the effect of his loss of honour. Eros is brought more into the picture, now with the queen, to prepare us for his crucial role with them both later.

Antony has now reached his lowest state. The realisation that he had betrayed himself shows him that he may also have to kill himself. 'I have lost my way for ever', 'I have fled myself', 'I have lost command', 'Let that be left which leaves itself', and so 'I have offended reputation', all within the first fifty lines. This is a masterly portrayal of a man driven out of his wits by distress, puzzled that Cleopatra still does not understand that his love for her compelled him to follow her 'fearful sails'. Surely, he says, you must have known:

How much you were my conqueror, and that
My sword, made weak by my affection, would
Obey it on all cause. (ll.65–8)

lated:	made late, delayed
loathness:	unwillingness
squares:	troop formations
beck:	call
palter:	bargain, dodge

Act III Scene 12

Caesar, however, is as cold in victory as he was before, refusing Antony's requests to remain in Egypt or in Athens as a private man, but instead bargaining with Cleopatra for him dead or alive, in exchange for her throne for her children. He then sends Thidias to 'try his cunning' and make promises in Caesar's name in order to win her from Antony, about whose conduct and bearing in defeat he wishes to know.

NOTES AND GLOSSARY:
The majesty of the court is stressed throughout the play by such casual references as the one here, 'superfluous kings for messengers' (I.5) and 'kings have been your fellows' (IV.2.13) by Antony to his servants, 'Three kings had I feasted' (II.2.80), and in the next scene also his 'kings would stand forth and cry 'Your will?'' (ll.91–2).

Shakespeare obliges himself to paint character in even such a minor part as this schoolmaster, a historical figure, whose scholarship is instantly revealed in his beautiful, modest simile (ll.8–10) of the dew on the myrtle, and his irresistible pun on 'lesson' (lessens) (l.13). Caesar's pitiless follow-up of his victory, his concentrated attack on the now weakened Cleopatra by trying to bribe her to betray Antony for the sake of her children's future, and the smooth, deceitful words from Thidias, again arouse our sympathy for Antony, and his frantic reactions of the next scene.

circle: crown
hazarded: dependent upon
bands: troops
vestal: Roman temple virgin

Act III Scene 13

In the palace Enobarbus, replying to the queen's question as to who is responsible for the tragedy, says that Antony was completely to blame, but he also implies that her power over Antony was the original cause.

Antony comes in and tells her of Caesar's terms, which he answers with a written challenge to fight him alone 'sword to sword'. This lunacy shocks Enobarbus because it shows that Caesar has conquered Antony's mind, too, and makes him question his own wisdom in remaining loyal to Antony.

Thidias enters and tells Cleopatra gently that Caesar realises that her opposition was due only to Antony, to which she agrees. Enobarbus is so shocked at this seeming betrayal that he goes to tell Antony, while Thidias continues to charm the queen. She says that she kisses Caesar's 'conquering hand', laying her crown at the feet of the 'universal landlord'. Rash Thidias, encouraged by this, asks if *he* may kiss *her* hand and stoops to do so. Antony enters upon this little intimacy and believes the worst. Furious also at the apparent disrespect of his servants he orders Thidias to be severely whipped and returned to Caesar. Bitter accusations about Cleopatra's infidelity, and scorn that she can 'mingle eyes' and fingers with an underling, precede his cry that this means 'the fall of Antony'. She pleads her faith so forcibly, swearing on the lives of her children, that he forgives her. When she quietly reveals that it is her birthday he gladly proposes that this shall be celebrated by one more gay night's revelry before he fights 'maliciously' the next day.

NOTES AND GLOSSARY:
This long scene is a playlet in itself: exposition of character and motives, the threatening deceit from outside, the discovery, then misunderstanding, the climax in violent action, recriminations, then resolution with forgiveness, to celebrate an optimisitic future. Antony's violence repeats, or balances, that of Cleopatra earlier towards her messenger, and each case is proof of their jealousy, fear of betrayal and so love. These indentical emotional reactions emphasise, therefore, the reasons for their mutual attraction.

As is to be expected, the wealth and variety of poetic expression increases with the intensified passions of the lovers in their distress: 'the rose of youth' (1.20), 'the blown rose' (1.39), 'the doom of Egypt' (1.78), 'By Jove that thunders' (1.85), 'Have I my pillow left unpressed?' (1.106), 'My play-fellow, your hand' (1.125), 'a morsel, cold upon dead Caesar's trencher' (1.116), 'our terrene moon is now eclipsed' (1.153), 'discandying' (1.165), 'There's sap in it yet' (1.191). We feel for them in their private hells, and Shakespeare with his usual economy of phrase shows how the strongest female emotions can be suggested by being left unspoken. Cleopatra's exclamation 'O!' (1.57) when Thidias has suggested that she acted only from fear of Antony, can be the key to the entire cause of the quarrel: her supposed betrayal. According to the interpretation of the director of the play and the inflection of the actress (or boy actor, in Shakespeare's time) a dozen different meanings can be offered: shock, surprise, denial, query, puzzlement, doubt, comprehension (of his motive), consideration, agreement, scorn, acceptance or simulated acceptance. If we accept Shakespeare's indication of the queen's character up to this moment as a shrewd, adoring and truly faithful paramour to Antony, then we can welcome the last meaning, which implies: 'Right, if you and Caesar really believe that, which I doubt, I will go along with you to find out his real intentions for us both.' Enobarbus and Antony misunderstand this and so the anger follows. Notice the conciliating patience of Cleopatra's short interjections, commencing only after thirty lines of Antony's rage: 'Good my Lord', 'O is't come to this?', 'wherefore is this?', and 'have you done yet?', 'not know me yet?' (1.157). At this Antony softens, and in two little words, short but drawn-out, 'Ah, dear' (1.158), she tenderly reassures him before passionately swearing to the gods that her love *is* true. Thidias is scornfully called a 'saucy jack', a nobody, a Jack-of-all-trades. This is a memory, surely, of the musical Sonnet 138 in which the ivory keys of the instrument his mistress is playing are personified as jacks

'that nimble leap to kiss the tender inward
of thy hand' . . . .
'Since *saucy* jacks so happy are in this
Give them thy fingers, me thy lips to kiss.'

Because Hipparchus (1.149) was the first of Antony's followers to desert, Antony's suggestion to use him is not an unreasonable joke. His new-spirit promise that 'I and my sword will earn our chronicle' (1.175), echoes what we have heard Enobarbus optimistically say in his own way (1.46). Even so, Antony's bravado that he will 'oustare the lightning' (1.194) is too much for his loyalty, and he realises that he can no longer stay with him.

ranges:	lines of warships
nicked:	cut into
comparisons:	comparable forces
parcel:	something similar to
haply:	perhaps
shroud:	protection
Jack:	rascal, low fellow
blasted:	withered, destroyed
feeders:	servants
boggler:	hesitater
Basan:	famous in the Bible
Hipparchus:	had deserted to Caesar
terrene:	earthly moon, that is, Cleopatra
points:	laces of clothing
discandying:	melting
gaudy:	gay
sap:	life
estridge:	a fierce bird

Act IV Scenes 1 and 2

Antony's insults and challenge are greeted by Caesar with scorn and laughter. He predicts that tomorrow will be the final battle, and so orders that his men are to be feasted, since he now has more than enough stores.

Once his challenge has been refused, Antony is determined to fight. He summons his servants and thanks them for their devotion, asking them to serve him as well as ever before at tonight's feast, since they may well have a new master tomorrow. Enobarbus complains to him that this 'discomfort' is making them all weep like women. Antony tries to laugh this off with forced humour to encourage them with a confident hope in his victory.

NOTES AND GLOSSARY:
Shakespeare cannot resist further contrasts between the rivals in these two scenes. Caesar faces Antony's hot rage with icy scorn, calling him the 'old ruffian', as though he were now harmless; so confident is he of the end of the campaign that his men can be feasted. Antony, on the other hand, will be 'bounteous at our meal' (1.10), thanking all his servants personally because *he* is not sure that he will survive the morrow.

This is the chain effect of grief subtly played by the poet: Antony's hints of death sadden everyone: the queen, Enobarbus and the several servants. This is an Antony they have never seen before, but one who is still so concerned with the welfare of others that as soon as he hears the rough words of Enobarbus he changes his mood and tries to comfort them, lightening his seriousness by jokingly using a striking poetic flower to turn sorrow to joy:

'Grace grow where these drops fall, my hearty friends' (1.38).

The herb of grace was another name for the plant rue, which means sorrow, pity or repentance, so Antony is making a pun.

make boot of: take advantage of
files: ranks
woo't: will you

Act IV Scene 3

Later that night when the Palace guard change, they talk hopefully of the next day's fight, but as they take up their positions a 'strange music' is heard in the air and beneath the ground. They interpret this fearfully as a sign that Antony is being abandoned by his patron, the god Hercules.

NOTES AND GLOSSARY:
This scene uses atmosphere effectively to add to the suspense of the audience about the future of the hero. The strange music, which in Plutarch accompanied a noise of people singing and dancing in a Bacchanalian procession, the darkness, the anxiety of the soldiers and the mention of the god, all contribute to the mystery. Shakespeare does not even mention that the procession was going out of the city to Caesar's camp.

Act IV Scene 4

Early the next morning Antony cheerfully leaves their bed and calls for Eros and his armour. Cleopatra, the 'armourer of his heart', nimbly and movingly helps him to put it on, and then is given a final 'soldier's kiss'. But although Antony goes out 'gallantly', 'like a man of steel', she wishes it were to fight Caesar alone.

NOTES AND GLOSSARY:
Antony's brisk gaiety as he prepares for battle affects us too. The bright early morning activity dismisses the gloom of the night before. This is, surprisingly, the first and only time that we see the principals together in intimate, loving mood with no argument. She is once more the adoring girl, pleased with her hero's compliments at her skill in arming him, which is better than that of his nervous squire Eros.

One of the reasons for the distance between the lovers is that the part of the queen was played by a boy in Shakespeare's theatre, so although the whole purpose for the play is their passion, he wisely never gives them time enough to develop it in front of us.

chuck: chick (affectionate term)
sooth: indeed
daff't: take it off, doff it
betimes: early
trim: armour
port: city gate

Act IV Scene 5

Just before the battle Antony is told by the old soldier that Enobarbus has deserted, but nevertheless he sends him 'gentle adieus and greetings' along with his treasure, regretting that his own fortunes have corrupted an honest man.

NOTES AND GLOSSARY:
The soldier here is the one who advised Antony not to fight by sea before Actium. His 'scars' ('these my wounds' in that scene, Act III.7.63) and Antony's apologies upon seeing him confirm this. It is ironical that it is he who announces the defection of Enobarbus, which has resulted, as Antony admits, from his own disregard of their advice. This is how the dramatist closely weaves his plot, strengthening our support for Antony by these two admissions of his guilt and his generosity to Enobarbus. Antony is so deeply moved at Enobarbus's weakness that he can only express his feelings by the single, heart-rent 'Enobarbus!' (l.18).

Act IV Scene 6

Caesar is now outside Alexandria, and in the hearing of Enobarbus commands that Antony is to be taken alive, but that those who have come over from him shall be placed in the front lines of battle to confuse him. Enobarbus, recalling the poor fortunes of others who have left their commanders, now realises that he can never enjoy life. This guilt is increased by the news that Antony has sent him his treasure, and so swearing that he can never fight against such a man, he vows that if his heart does not break now, then he will go and die suitably in some ditch.

NOTES AND GLOSSARY:
Caesar's policy of merciless executions and his placing of deserters in the front line, as well as Enobarbus's repentance, further emphasise

Antony's generosity, 'thou mine of bounty'. Reading 'despair' for 'thought' in line 34 makes the heart-break of Enobarbus, now the self-confessed 'villain of the earth', more understandable.

three-nooked:	three-cornered
vant:	front
turpitude:	unworthiness
blows:	explodes

Act IV Scenes 7 and 8

The cavalry engagement is won by Antony, and Scarus (back with him again, in spite of Actium) is wounded as they beat Agrippa and Caesar back 'to their beds'. Antony praises his men and, overjoyed at his success, begs the queen to embrace him, armour and all, and then to 'leap into his heart'. Scarus is commended and commanded to kiss the hand of Cleopatra who rewards him with a king's golden suit of armour, before the joyful couple celebrate victory with a triumphant march through the city.

NOTES AND GLOSSARY:
The short scenes stress the speed of events, the results of which are expanded in the longer ones. Antony's care for the wounded Scarus and his praise of him to the queen keep before us his constant consideration for others, as well as his boyish delight at his own unexpected success. This he immediately shares with Cleopatra, his 'nightingale' (1.18), his 'great fairy' (1.12), the enchantress who has brought him such luck. This is the general Marcus Antonius of old, 'the greatest soldier of the world', gaily celebrating victory, and applauded by official fanfares—but for the last time.

clouts:	blows, and cloths
bench-holes:	latrines
scotches:	gashes
gests:	deeds, actions
doughty-handed:	bold
clip:	embrace, hug
fairy:	enchanting lady
carbuncled:	jewelled
carouses:	full cups of wine
tabourines:	drums

Act IV Scene 9

Later that night sentries in Caesar's camp overhear someone praying to the moon to shatter his heart with the flint-hardness of his guilt, so that he may die, and begging Antony to forgive him. Going to speak to him, they find Enobarbus, who has killed himself.

NOTES AND GLOSSARY:
The farewell invocation to the moon by Enobarbus, 'O sovereign mistress of true melancholy' (l.12), reminds us of Antony's reference to Cleopatra as 'O terrene moon', since she was the incarnation of Isis, the moon-goddess. Enobarbus may well feel that she, as Antony's love, has been the instrument of both his and Antony's 'melancholy' downfall, which caused his worthless betrayal of friendship. He is the first of the principals to die, and all finally for the same reasons: their preference for love and loyalty in Egypt, in opposition to the calculating self-interest of Caesar in Rome.

to's:	for us
disponge:	drip (from a sponge)
foot:	foot soldiers

Act IV Scenes 10 and 11

The next day Antony is prepared for battle by both land and sea, and goes with Scarus to the high ground above the harbour to observe the action. But Caesar orders his men to hold their positions, and not to fight by land unless attacked, which he thinks unlikely, because Antony's best men are in his ships.

Act IV Scenes 12 and 13

Now Antony climbs higher to the pine tree to get a better view. Scarus has just disclosed that birds nesting in the ships' sails are an unfavourable omen when Antony bursts in wildly, cursing Cleopatra for betraying him.

The fleet has surrendered; the only thing left for him to do now is to be revenged on her, so all others can flee. Cleopatra comes in as he is accusing her of tricking him into complete ruin, but he shouts at her to disappear like the witch she must be. He says he would kill her, but this would deprive Caesar of her for his triumph. No, it would be better punishment for her to be displayed to the mob as a monster, and for Octavia's nails to scratch her face. This terrifies the queen so much that she rushes away to hide in her unfinished tomb, while Antony calls upon his ancestor Hercules to help him to kill himself, after he has slain Cleopatra for selling him to Caesar.

In scene 13 Cleopatra goes to the monument with her women, and, at Charmian's suggestion, instructs Mardian to tell Antony that she has killed herself and died with his name on her lips.

NOTES AND GLOSSARY:

This is the last battle, in which Antony is ruined not by Caesar but by his mistaken belief that Cleopatra has once more betrayed him. It is this lack of sufficient faith on his part that causes the train of events that takes them both to death. His rage makes her run away and then try to win him back with a last, typical, trick or 'spell', by sending false news of her death, so it is she who betrays him into such deep despair that he commits suicide.

Scene 12 is mainly one long speech by the frantic Antony, except for the few lines from Scarus about the swallows, and a single one from the queen. Her supernatural power over him is emphasised by the mention of the augurers, and the insults he hurls at her. Lines 17–29, from 'O sun', are pathetic but beautiful. The stream of metaphorical personifications and adjectives vividly describe his feelings of utter 'loss', at being abandoned by everyone, most of all by her for whom he has given his all.

We notice the increasing use of physical elements in his words, accentuated as he realises that death will soon take away his senses. He will 'see' the sun no more, 'shake hands' with victor fortune, while 'the hearts' of his followers, who have been faithful spaniels at his 'heels', are now melting like tasty, discandied 'sweets' on Caesar, 'blossoming', like a flower, while he the tallest 'pine' tree of them all has his glories ('bark') stripped from him. 'Betrayed' by the 'soul' of Egypt, whose 'eye', both its beauty and its power, made him fight and run from Actium, and whose 'bosom' (love) was his sole, crowning objective, he has been tricked to the 'very heart' of deepest defeat.

pine:	tree
tripled-turned:	having loved three men
charm:	enchantress
spell:	magic influence
avaunt:	get away
dolts:	fools
Nessus:	Centaur poisoned by Hercules
Lichas:	attendant of Hercules who brought the poisoned shirt
lodge:	impale
Telamon:	father of Ajax
embossed:	foaming at the mouth

Act IV Scene 14

We find a calmer Antony now talking with Eros in the palace about his disillusionment with Cleopatra, for whom he has fought the wars, but because of whose betrayal he is not himself, and so must end his life. Mardian arrives and, on being told that the queen must die, replies that she has already killed herself. Antony, therefore, instantly decides that he must follow her. As he unbuckles the armour she so recently fastened on, he calls upon her to wait in heaven for him, where hand in hand they will amaze all the spirits with the strength of their love. Explaining how Cleopatra's brave deed has now dishonoured him, he says that the time has now come for Eros to keep the promise, sworn when Antony freed him, that he would kill his master if this ever became necessary. Eros protests, but when Antony insists, stabs himself. This shames Antony into falling upon his sword, which only wounds him. When no one will make the final thrust he is carried, dying, to Cleopatra in the monument, having heard from Diomed that, after all, she is not dead.

NOTES AND GLOSSARY:
The unfamiliar calm of Antony, resigned, at last, to the finality of his situation, is changed to urgency by the news of Cleopatra's death. That terrible, single syllable, 'Dead' (l.34), is an echoing of Antony's same word to Enobarbus (I.2.149) telling of the death of his other wife, Fulvia. It takes readers of *Julius Caesar* back further to the evening before Philippi when Brutus calms the angry Cassius with similar news of the death of his wife Portia (*Julius Caesar* IV.3).

Typically, Antony holds himself responsible, and so he must waste no time before rejoining her, to weep for his pardon (l.45). The pathos of the self-sacrifice of Eros, (a devotion which neither Cassius nor Brutus could command at their suicides); Antony's affectionate anxiety for him: 'weep not, Gentle Eros' (l.21), 'put colour in thy cheek' (l.69); the refusal of all his other followers to 'despatch' him, and his gentle thanks to them for carrying him, uncomplaining, and once more forgiving, to Cleopatra, all make this, for us, Antony's finest, most heroic hour.

dislims:	changes shape
moe:	more
Ajax:	his shield had seven layers of leather
case:	body
port:	bearing
Aeneas:	he visited Dido after her suicide
troops:	followers
Parthian darts:	Parthian arrows
pleached:	folded
pole:	standard
jewel:	Antony

Act IV Scene 15

Cleopatra, horrified to see Antony dying, but apologising for not letting him in, for fear of capture, hauls him up to the window, with her ladies. If she could revive him now by kissing, she says she would wear out her lips. He calls for wine and tells her to make an honourable deal with Caesar, but warns her to trust no one but Proculeius. She replies that she trusts only her determination to follow him. Dying, now, he begs her not to grieve at his death, but rather to recall his past glories and rejoice that he dies nobly, overcome only by himself, a Roman. She faints when she sees that he has died, and now since 'there is nothing left remarkable' to live for, she says they will bury him, be brave and then by their suicide in the 'high Roman fashion' 'make death proud to take' them, too.

NOTES AND GLOSSARY:
The power of the poetry increases, as the spirit-lamps go out (1.85), and the suggestive imagery of Shakespeare's melting metaphors in this and the final scene of the queen's death have not been bettered anywhere. Here Antony's sure love for her, proved by his actions in the former scene, is now matched by her passion for him, expressed in her despairing words, 'Hast thou no care of me?' (1.60), as he dies in her arms. There is no other love/death scene like this in all Shakespeare. As the hero ascends to 'where souls do couch on flowers' (IV.14.51), he passes to her, his heroine, a mantle of nobility which will now strengthen her resolve to defy Caesar.

Act V Scene 1

Just after Caesar has sent Dolabella to command the surrender of Antony, Decretas brings the news of his suicide, presenting the blood-stained sword as proof. This saddens them all, and Caesar apparently weeps as he praises Antony, his 'mate in empire', saying that the death of so great a man should have made a louder noise. This speech is interrupted by a messenger from Cleopatra, whom he assures of good treatment. Now Proculeius, whom Antony mentioned, is sent to comfort the queen so that her possible suicide will not spoil Caesar's triumph, and to report on her present condition.

NOTES AND GLOSSARY:
Antony, being dead, cannot come to impatient Caesar, but his sword, the symbol of his power and manhood, is handed over by Decretas, who loudly praises his former master before bravely offering his services to Caesar. Caesar's formal, grand remark that great Antony's

death should have made a greater thunder, since he was half the world (l.19), emphasises that it leaves the other half, that is himself, now the 'sole sir o' the world' (V.2.120).

Shakespeare keeps Caesar still in his cool character even at these 'tidings to wash the eyes of kings' (l.28). For only after his two ministers have warmly praised Antony does he proclaim, with little genuine regret, a formal justification for his actions, working up to a forced, insincere-sounding list of compliments, before he is gladly able to hear the queen's messenger.

doom: death
moiety: half
meeter: more suitable

Act V Scene 2

Desolate Cleopatra now has the compensation of appreciating more the final worthlessness of her former glory. This is illustrated by the certainty that even Caesar, now triumphant, is still the servant of Fate. And she feels relief and pride at making her firm decision to do the final deed, to die, never again to taste dung-grown food, which in their common need makes Caesar equal with a beggar. While Proculeius falsely assures her of Caesar's good intentions, and she asks that her son may rule after her, Gallus has entered the tomb with soldiers, and her instant attempt to stab herself is prevented. Nevertheless, she insists to Proculeius that she will starve to death or be hung in chains from the pyramids rather than be displayed in Caesar's triumph. Dolabella now comes to guard her, and he is so enchanted by her description of her dream of Antony that he reveals that Caesar does intend to 'lead her in triumph'. At this Caesar comes in, confirming it by the threat that if she kills herself he will execute her children. She tries to convince him that she will stay alive, by admitting she kept back half her treasure to help to finance her survival. For exposing this deception she attacks her steward Seleucus brutally, and apologises to Caesar, who, while forgiving her dishonesty, urges her to eat and sleep well. This convinces the queen of his deceit, and when Dolabella confirms it with the official news that she and her children are to be sent ahead in three days to Rome, she hardens the resolve of her women by describing their indignities in the proposed triumph. Then she calls for her 'best attires', in which to meet Antony again, as at Cydnus.

The clown (rustic) brings in the basket of figs, and extends the suspense with salty, comic comments about women and 'the worm', and we now have the moving scene of their deaths. Cleopatra anticipates for us her meeting, at last, with 'her husband', and vividly describes the physical feelings induced by her elation.

She kisses farewell to Iras, who falls dead, which characteristically makes the queen anxious to claim that kiss of welcome from Antony before Iras. So she quickly puts the poisonous snake to her breast, thus fooling Caesar, and comparing it to the baby sucking the nurse asleep.

She dies, calling on Antony. Charmian closes her eyes, adjusts her crown, and then herself takes a snake. Just as she dies, the guards burst in, followed by Dolabella and Caesar. He accepts that she has bravely outwitted him, and they deduce from the marks on the bodies and fig leaves the cause of death. Caesar commands that the famous pair shall be buried together, and announces that after the solemn state funeral he will return to Rome.

NOTES AND GLOSSARY:

The entire scene is Cleopatra's; she has the whole of the action. Several swift episodes are linked by the intelligent determination and royal bearing of the queen, who is the cause and centre of the excitement. To the end she is mistress of the situation and we are shown the serpentine course by which her love achieves her death. Recognising that even the greatest queen and lover is dependent, just as Caesar is, upon Fortune, she knows that to attain a finer life with Antony she must terminate the present one. When she is sure, from Caesar's manner, that she is for Rome, she prepares herself serenely for death, which will bring release from Caesar and unity with Antony. With all deception spent and her delight that she has fooled Caesar, the full majesty of the new, inspired queen is shown in her dignified approach to and eager acceptance, as a bride, of death. In a glorious climax of immortal verse, she comes to consummation with her husband, the 'curléd Antony, 'noblest of men', and Shakespeare achieves the culmination of his career as a dramatist of love.

pinioned:	prisoner, as of a bird with clipped wings
varletry:	mob
abhorring:	a decaying mess
scutcheons:	coats of arms
vouchsafing:	condescending
immoment:	insignificant
Livia:	Caesar's wife
hie:	hurry
lictors:	Roman officials
aspic:	poison of the asp
unpolicied:	outwitted
awry:	out of place
toil of grace:	snare of beauty
blown:	swollen
vent:	discharge

Part 3

Commentary

Alexandria, known always as The City, was founded by Alexander the Great in 332BC, and remained the capital of Egypt for more than a thousand years. At the time of Cleopatra it had reached the peak of its glory. Alexander's wisdom had borne fruit, because the harbours on both the sea and the great Lake Mariout, between the town and the interior of Egypt, had now made it the world's most prosperous port. It was also a centre of culture of unique splendour, housing approximately three hundred thousand citizens and even more slaves. The City, we should remember, was primarily Greek, like its queen, Cleopatra, who was descended from the first Ptolemy. This Macedonian general had been the close friend and also the biographer of Alexander, upon whose death in 323BC he wisely took Egypt, as his share of the Empire. As Ptolemy I Soter (the Saviour) he became the first Greek Pharaoh, after Alexander, from 305-282BC. Our Cleopatra VII was the last (51-30BC).

The characters

Cleopatra and Julius Caesar

For our understanding of the play Roman-Egyptian history begins with Julius Caesar (100-44BC). The story of his arrival, during the Civil War, his meeting with the young Cleopatra, his battles in Alexandria, and the final establishment of her as queen, and his mistress, is known from the histories, but also told amusingly, if inaccurately, by Bernard Shaw, in his play and film *Caesar and Cleopatra*. Caesar's struggle for control of Rome was against the father of the Sextus Pompey in this play, known as Pompey the Great. He was treacherously murdered as he landed in Egypt in 48BC by Roman officers, on the orders of Cleopatra's brother, the young King Ptolemy XIII. Pompey was coming to Egypt for help and money after his defeat by Caesar at Pharsalia in Greece. When Caesar arrived in Alexandria four days later he was handed the embalmed head and ring of Pompey.

Now when Caesar in his turn was murdered in 44BC, Cleopatra was there in Rome with their three-year-old son Caesarion. Mark Antony was joint consul with Caesar that year. And it was Antony's offer of the crown to him that had so angered Brutus and Cassius, and then his clever words and popularity that turned the people against them, leaving him the most important man in Rome, at the age of thirty-nine.

Cleopatra had long ago realised, as she grew to political maturity, that to restore Egypt to its former glory she must have the help of Rome. Caesar came to Egypt chasing Pompey, but also chasing money, because it was the richest country in the world. So he must have been satisfied when he won the whole country, and its fascinating twenty-one-year-old queen as well.

Cleopatra was small, of dark, not black, complexion, since she was Greek, with possibly reddish-brown hair, petite, lithe, exceptionally lively and intellectually stimulating. To the experienced Caesar, 'the most powerful and intelligent leader' Rome had ever produced, she must have seemed to radiate a very special charm. Shakespeare indicates this to us, as she thinks aloud about absent Antony:

> Broad-fronted Caesar
> When thou wast here above ground, I was
> A morsel for a monarch: (I.5.29–31)

But those were her 'salad days', when she was inexperienced, she admits, 'green in judgement' and 'cold in blood' (I.5.73–4). Even so, as Agrippa admiringly cries out, interrupting Enobarbus's description of her at Cydnus:

> Royal Wench!
> She made great Caesar lay his sword to bed:
> He ploughed her, and she cropped. (II.2.229).

We see how powerful the metaphors are here, each idea urging Shakespeare's thoughts faster forward. When peace comes the weapons are forged into the plough-shares to bring the battle-fields to harvest, so Caesar's sword, potent in bed, was the instrument of the queen's fertility. It is, ironically, Sextus Pompey who later, in another suggestive metaphor, speaks of 'Egyptian cookery' and 'I have heard that Julius Caesar/grew fat with feasting there' (II.6.64). He even brings up the well-known story of the queen's first appearance before Caesar in Alexandria rolled up in a mattress (ll.68–70). Later Cleopatra, when offering her hand to Thidias, envoy from victorious Octavius, says provocatively

> 'Your Caesar's father oft,
> When he hath mused of taking kingdoms in,
> Bestowed his lips on that unworthy place,
> As it rained kisses.' (III.13.82)

When Antony bitterly brings up her previous loves, Shakespeare makes him repeat her earlier metaphor:

'I found you a morsel, cold upon
Dead Caesar's trencher; nay, you were a fragment
Of Cnaeus Pompey's, besides what hotter hours,
Unregistered in vulgar fame, you have
Luxuriously picked out.' (l.116)

Here all of them, Plutarch, Shakespeare and his Antony, reveal the force of the fierce anti-Cleopatra propaganda so effectively put out by Octavian's agents and historians in Rome. No woman in history has suffered so much from unfounded sexual slander and libel ('vulgar fame' above). Cnaeus Pompey had visited Egypt with his father years before and although Cleopatra recalls how he anchored 'his aspect' and 'made his eyes grow' in her brows (I.5.32) there is no evidence of a closer relationship, certainly nothing worse than that which Antony, like any doubting lover, might throw out in the heat of a quarrel.

The problem of Cleopatra, in fact, and in our understanding of the play, has been caused largely by the lack of sure contemporary portraits and accounts of her appearance, character and actions. A woman is always most vulnerable in the area of her moral reputation, and the vicious distortion of the truth has clouded posterity's and our visions, and unfairly hidden her many other accomplishments, proved by the fact that she was associated with the two most popular rulers of the world's most powerful nation. She was a super-civilised Greek, but to the Romans she was a 'damned foreigner', from the barbaric East, and weirdly mysterious Egypt, which frightened them out of their superstitious wits. Against this intelligent, ambitious politician, who also happened to be a faithful consort and dedicated mother,

'was launched one of the most terrible outbursts of hatred in history; no accusation was too vile to be hurled at her, and the charges which were made have echoed through the world ever since, and have sometimes been taken for facts.'*

So when Caesar fell, from the twenty-three 'envious dagger' thrusts of the assassins, it was no wonder that Cleopatra felt she should slip quietly away with their son from a Rome in chaos. Her dreams of a wider world, a peaceful Middle East Empire, secured and ruled over by them both, possibly from Alexandria, was now destroyed. But in the vigorous Antony, who now took over Caesar's purple mantle, and who, as his friend, had probably helped her to escape, she was to find a companion with similar liberal and international ideals, and from their association Shakespeare fashioned the drama of his play.

*W.W. Tarn & M.P. Charlesworth, *Octavian, Antony and Cleopatra*, Cambridge University Press, Cambridge, 1965, p.98.

Julius Caesar and Antony

For dramatic purposes, Shakespeare made Julius Caesar unattractive:
an irritable, arrogant, vain and self-satisfied dictator: 'I am constant as
the northern star', and 'know that Caesar doth not wrong'. But he is
fond of and relies upon the younger Antony, who, unlike Cassius,
'loves plays'. They have been friends and colleagues for several years,
alike in many characteristics: brilliant generalship, care for and devotion from their men, yet also possessing a keen appreciation of women,
and a driving delight in the honour and power which success brings.

Shakespeare speaks his true opinion of Caesar from the lips of
Antony, in his funeral oration, which, though not in Plutarch, has
echoed down the ages. Thus the seemingly blunt but subtle Antony, in
his determined avenging of Caesar's murder, succeeds him, both as
the new master of the Roman world, and also as the heir to Cleopatra's
kingdom and her love.

Antony and Octavius Caesar

Julius Caesar had mentioned neither Cleopatra nor Caesarion in his
official will, having named rather a Roman, his grand-nephew Octavius,
as his heir and his adopted son. Octavius was then an unknown, delicate
youth aged nineteen, in training in Apollonia (present-day Albania),
preparing for Caesar's great campaign against the Parthians, which he
had planned to start three days after the Ides of March. Antony was
then double the age of Octavius, and the struggle for power between
them began from the moment the young man arrived in Rome, only
to be ended fourteen years later by Antony's suicide. Neither could
trust the other, and their first armed encounter was at Modena, where
Antony was already besieging the conspirator Decimus Brutus.
Octavius, whose own plot to have Antony murdered had been dis-
covered, raised an army and actually went to the defence of his uncle's
murderer, and with the two new consuls Hirtus and Pansa defeated the
avenging Antony. But it was said that Octavius engineered the deaths
of the two consuls in order to obtain their armies. In our play Shakespeare makes Octavius quote the incident, both to praise Antony's
courage, but also to suggest that it was he who had killed the consuls
(I.4.56). Eventually, however, with Marcus Lepidus they formed the
Second Triumvirate to concentrate on defeating Caesar's chief mur-
derers, at Philippi in 42BC. This is told in the second part of *Julius
Caesar*, where in his few lines he is clearly made arrogant and aggressive
towards Antony. Octavius did not distinguish himself at Philippi,
where according to the Roman historian Suetonius, but not according
to Shakespeare, his brutal treatment of the prisoners so disgusted the

survivors that while they courteously saluted Antony as their conqueror they insulted Octavius to his face 'with the most obscene epithets'. Antony, then, at the division of the empire, having chosen to pacify the richest, eastern part, went to Athens and then to Asia (Turkey). He summoned Cleopatra to Tarsus, on the river Cydnus, to query her conduct against the conspirators, but mainly to request her aid in his Parthian campaign. The result of their meeting makes the play.

Power was possible in those days, just as now, only if it was backed by armies, which had to be paid, to fight for the money to pay them. Pompey and Caesar both went to Egypt for money to finance their forces, and both lost their heads there. Antony and Octavius quarrelled over money, land, ships and soldiers. Antony chose the east as his area because to conquer the Parthians and other Eastern kingdoms would bring gold with the glory, and because of fabulously wealthy Egypt. And Octavius, finally, followed Antony to Egypt more to fill his treasury with Cleopatra's riches than to lead her in triumph through Rome. Behind the high human figures in these fifteen years of drama were, therefore, always the golden treasure-vaults of the East and Egypt. Julius Caesar and the queen, with their heir Caesarion, could have ruled as Cleopatra had hoped, as monarchs of a greater Graeco-Roman empire stretching from Britain to India, larger even than the realm of Alexander. But the prophetic books in Rome said that only a Roman *king* could conquer the Parthians, and Antony had offered Caesar the crown, and Caesar had died for it. Caius Julius had died and Caius Octavius was his avenged Roman heir. But still there was Caesar's natural son, Caesarion, and his mother, the Queen of Egypt, who was now the sacred wife of Antony, Caesar's acknowledged successor in experienced generalship, with the same international ambitions. Octavius was no fool, being aware of all this, but also of the widespread love and loyalty which Antony still commanded in Italy.

So he planned coolly and ruthlessly, while Antony with his trusting and generous nature gave him time and opportunity.

By comparing what Antony did historically with his words and actions in the play we can see where Shakespeare's skill lies.

In Athens, as hero of the day, Antony was at home, for here he had studied his speech-making (recently so effectively practised in Rome), in the 'Asiatic', forceful, uninhibited style, and he genuinely loved Greek culture.

Antony and Cleopatra as gods

Over in Turkey, in the Greek city of Ephesus, a significant event happened to Antony. No one man had had so wide a control of the East, since Alexander, who had tactfully been identified with the god, when he had offered to rebuild the famous Temple of Artemis (Diana) in 324BC. So Antony was now declared to be the New Dionysus, the universal god of the Hellenistic Age. Octavius might be the 'son' of the recently deified Caesar but Antony was now a god himself, the son they proclaimed, of Mars and Venus. Dionysus was, of course, Bacchus the lawgiver, and lover of peace, who taught men to cultivate the vine throughout all Asia and in Egypt.

A clear idea of the degrees of divinity assumed in the play by the three principals is needed for our understanding of all its implications. Today, when so little remains sacred, this has to be a conscious effort. Cleopatra was trained as a priestess of Isis, but being the daughter of Ptolemy Auletes, who had, himself, been styled the new Dionysus, she was a goddess in her own right before she even ascended the throne.

Just as European monarchs and their peoples in Shakespeare's time believed in the divine right of kings, so to Egypt, and to Cleopatra, she was herself the goddess Isis, and Caesarion, as her son, was Horus. Isis, one of the most ancient goddesses, was the most popular and beloved of all Egyptian deities and the greatest of all protective divinities, also, in the Graeco-Roman world. Her worship had spread beyond the east from the Sahara to Britain on a sensational scale. Isis offered her devotees forgiveness, communion with the deity, and immortality. She worked through ritual dreams ('Emperor Antony', V.2.76) and the priestly interpretation of visions (the soothsayer), and became the supreme enchantress of Egypt ('great fairy'), sorceress ('charm', 'spell') 'of great magic'. Isis was assimilated with almost all goddesses throughout the Nile valley, and elsewhere was identified with Aphrodite; she was the deity of women, the goddess of love and fertility, of the earth and all its fruits, the sea, the Nile, the moon and life beyond the grave. So the creative vividness of Shakespeare's metaphors and his choice of rich liquid imagery can be seen to be correctly based.

The husband and brother of Isis was Osiris. His familiar legend suggested that he was a King of Egypt, travelling into foreign lands, spreading the blessings of civilisation. He was murdered by his evil brother Set, cut up and thrown into the Nile. After a long search Isis found his remains and later defeated, and regained the sovereign power from Set. The religious aspect of Cleopatra's marriage to her brother Ptolemy is now understandable, as following the Pharaonic custom. For Isis-Cleopatra, then, Julius Caesar had been her Osiris, and Caesarion Horus. But the new-found Osiris was Antony; thus both her unions were *sacred marriages of Gods on earth*, linking Egypt with Greece and with Rome.

So both Cleopatra and Octavius feel threatened by each other, and theirs is a divine struggle for survival. When, therefore, the queen received Antony's summons to Tarsus, she planned and stage-managed their first meeting brilliantly. Here was Isis-Aphrodite-Venus come to meet and revel with Dionysus-Bacchus-Hercules, and to find in him the new Osiris. Antony had recently even decreed a new shrine for the worship of Isis in Rome, and so Cleopatra knew that he was spiritually favourable and physically highly susceptible.

Cleopatra and Antony: appearance

Isis was queen of the rivers, winds and sea, so by these in 41BC Cleopatra sailed in her solar barge up the Phoenician coast to Cydnus and her destiny. Her female power penetrated space and time, and cast such a spell first on Antony, and then on Plutarch and Shakespeare, that she inspired what has come to be considered the playwright's supreme passage of descriptive poetry (II.2.193). Antony was caught, for although Cleopatra was, as Isis, mother of the universe and mistress of nature, as Venus she was a woman determined, as only Cleopatra could be, to get her helpmate. How simply Shakespeare solves the problem of her physical features, by using the now all-embracing, familiar phrase:

> For her person,
> It beggared all description . . .
> O'er picturing that Venus where we see
> The fancy outwork nature.

She was, in fact, 'Too marvellous for words', larger or lovelier than life. This is an aspect of Shakespeare's universality, his expression from his own experience, that the imagined, the anticipated, is more exquisite than reality. Cleopatra must have made the most of what nature and her parents gave her: auburn hair styled by her hair-dresser Iras, provocative nose, intense brown eyes (Pompey, I.5.31), generous mouth ('Eternity was in our lips and eyes'), firm chin and slim, sinuous figure. She was then twenty-nine years old, at the height of physical and intellectual attractiveness, and potent with an irrestible vitality.

Antony

The aristocratic Antony—general, orator, sportsman, 'masquer and reveller'—was both a man's man, for his soldiers, and a ladies' man, who could never say 'no' to a woman; but was as well able to endure the hard life of campaigning as the good life of peace-time society. How did he look this day, 'enthroned' in the market place at Tarsus?

He was a tall, large, solid man, with a head of curly hair and beard, 'barbered ten times over', accentuating his masculine features. This imposing appearance helped to support his belief in his descent from the hero-god Hercules, who was closely connected with Dionysus (as both were with Alexander the Great). Hercules was also a unifier of the world, the symbol of concord between Greek and Roman societies.

But it was not only the physical looks of these magnificent beings but their charms of personality which held them obsessed, through the most extreme stresses, during the next eleven years.

Cleopatra's character

Cleopatra brought to this unique association of two exceptional spirits in 'the tide of time' a royal heritage, a training as a monarch and high priestess, along with the courage, political and administrative skills required for personal and dynastic survival, combined in a majesty accustomed to command, to obedience, and so to flattery. She was keenly intelligent, highly talented, well educated and widely read (she is said to have got her chief pleasure from literature), and curious about and involved in the arts and sciences which flourished in her capital. Fluent in many languages, she was the first Ptolemy to master Egyptian. With her beautiful voice she was a witty and stimulating talker, mistress of all courtly, social graces and feminine charms.

So it is Shakespeare's expression of these qualities in his womanly queen, suggested by Plutarch's pages, that make Cleopatra his 'most amazing and dazzling single personification'.*

We see her being in turn proud, humble, a clawing tigress, a teasing, fainting teenager; regal, skittish, priestly, cunningly deceitful and yet faithful even to death: in fact, the epitome of the female character. When threatened she can be excitable, hysterical, aggressive, pitiless and inhuman, but as a wife and mother she is warm, tender, gentle, unselfish, and alluringly lovable. She is restless, moody, sad, tense, changeable, irritable when waiting, bored, for Antony, but once with him relaxed, gay, eager, impulsive, reasonable and graciously attentive. What a provocative, exasperating concentration of film-star temperament, what a puzzling, contradictory blending of diversity and joy! Cleopatra was a rainbow spectrum of humanity, a challenge indeed for those two greatest soldiers and tacticians whom she bewitched.

Antony's character

Until Antony's selfconfident optimism and abused loyalty undid him he was a great soldier and tactician. His special power was that he could get the most and the best out of his followers, because they all considered themselves to be his friends. Ferocious, leonine courage (Philippi, Alexandria), determination, hardihood under physical and

*G. Wilson Knight, *The Imperial Theme*, Methuen, London, 1965, p.289.

mental stresses (Modena, Parthia and Actium) were mixed with faith, trust and forgiveness.

Patrician but not proud, he displayed, as a big-boned military commander, a swaggering appearance, a bravado of natural conscious strength. All things to all men, and to all women, he was a sincere, easy mixer, enjoying equally sophisticated court carousals ('Three kings had I newly feasted', II.2.80), as well as ribald mess-room guzzles with his soldiers ('to sit and keep the turn of tippling with a slave', I.4.18). He unashamedly enjoyed his attraction to and for women ('the beds i' the East are soft', II.6.50), and for other more peaceful entertainments of the flesh. His keen, bluff, and probably earthy sense of humour gave him the much-loved ability to laugh, even at himself, and when convinced of his mistakes to admit them unstintingly.

He came to Cleopatra as a heavily 'married' man, who had already fathered children on the extraordinary Fulvia, 'a greater political force than any Roman woman had ever been before, and the first wife of a Roman leader and ruler ever to play a really active part in political life'.* So he could play the domestic diplomat as well as Cleopatra, could be gentle and considerate ('My precious Queen', 'most sweet Queen', 'fall not a tear'), courtly and gay ('What sport tonight?'), extravagant and attentive, when required. No doubt she appreciated his deep-voiced compliments and calculating generosity. After all he gave to Enobarbus his treasure-chests, to his followers his treasure-ship, while to her he gave kingdoms, forgiveness and finally his life. So these were the two paramount rulers now allied in both person and politics, who returned to winter in Alexandria, Antony's new headquarters for the Parthian war. It was the sudden advance of these Parthians which took him from spring-time Egypt into Asia Minor, where he heard the grave news of Fulvia's war on Caesar. Over in Athens he found his mother with the defeated Fulvia, whom he must have sternly reproached for putting at further risk his alliance with Caesar. Sextus Pompey's hospitality to the mother, and Fulvia's death shortly after in Sicyon, are mentioned, out of time, in the play. And since Antony now went straight over to Italy with his army to sign the Treaty of Brindisi with Lepidus and Caesar, we can see how Shakespeare has already juggled with history in the early scenes of the play, correctly using Caesar's arrogance and Fulvia's dominance to emphasise Cleopatra's jealousy and instinctive fear of letting Antony return to Rome.

Octavius Caesar, Octavia and Antony

Octavius was then a slight, handsome young man of twenty-three, but already experienced in the cruelty of survival. His suspicions and fears

* Michael Grant, *Cleopatra*, Panther, London, 1974, p.177.

of Antony, now so closely connected with the powerful, wealthy mother of Caesar's son, both perpetual threats to his position, can be understood. He planned much further ahead than Antony. So, since he would gain, whatever happened afterwards, he now sacrificed his sister to his ambitions, by agreeing to her marriage with Antony. What Shakespeare does not reveal is that this domestic back-up to signed treaties was customary, and that Octavius had himself already married Clodia, Antony's step-daughter by Fulvia, to seal the Second Triumvirate. But Antony's soldiers and the whole war-sick Roman world desired his marriage with Octavia, hoping it would ensure a peace.

Octavia appears to have been a paragon of virtue. She was in her twenties, lovely to look at, tall and fair, a calm, dignified figure but with active intellectual interests. She was the patron of Maecenas, her brother's friend and minister, who himself was famous as the patron of Virgil and Horace. Shakespeare, being so dependent upon and grateful for the help of his own patron, must have appreciated this aspect of her character. 'Patient' Octavia was a devoted and loyal wife to Antony, and a remarkable mother to his other children, in addition to their own; she was beyond reproach as the wife of Caesar's successor, and a loving sister of Caesar's heir.

But how long could her 'beauty, wisdom and modesty' (II.2.244) hold Antony to his Western alliance? To the credit of both husband and wife, in spite of what Enobarbus called her 'holy, cold and still conversation' (II.6.118), it survived those four years which Shakespeare cunningly cuts down to little more than a weekend honeymoon. His play demands speed, contrast and balance, and by this drastic reduction he can sustain the intrigue. So in the middle of the grim, hard-faced Roman arguments and political underpinning Shakespeare explodes into the scene his poetic bombshell—the Enobarbus description of the new husband's meeting with his mistress at Tarsus.

As if this were not enough, he immediately reinforces the power of the queen, by bringing the soothsayer into the next scene. He is our link with the court, and he has further ominous truths to tell, pointing to the coming tragedy, about Caesar's superior spirit. The message from Cleopatra is that Antony should return to her, and he takes this hint, by admitting that whatever the motives were for his wedding they crumble at the call of the queen. So we have the well-meaning victims of a universal wish for peace, Antony and Octavia, crushed by the stronger, selfish ambitions of East-Cleopatra and West-Caesar. But Antony could not leave Italy yet, because Pompey had to be checked by the Misenum pact, around the celebration of which Shakespeare creates one of his most unusual scenes, revealing subtly, in little more than a hundred quick, effective lines, character impressions of each of the rulers of the Roman world. Lepidus is a drunken bore, Pompey a cynical hypocrite, Caesar a wet blanket and poor party man, while Antony, witty, relaxed and benevolent, is in his element, as Dionysus, in the drinking-song and dance. But such a flimsy treaty could not endure. Caesar and Antony together finished off Pompey, but not until four years later, in 36BC.

With their first daughter, Antony and Octavia now spent eighteen months' holiday in Athens, as important state visitors, and it was from his headquarters there that Antony sent Publius Ventidius to push the Parthians back. Ventidius, a brilliant general, achieved this, but at grave cost to himself, and later to Antony, a fact that Shakespeare does not mention. He makes Ventidius critical of both Antony and Caesar (III.1), but fails to add that because he so unsuccessfully bribed an enemy city Antony had to go and reduce it himself. This meant that Antony could never again trust or use Ventidius. He and Agrippa were Rome's top-flight generals and it was the latter's seizure of Antony's bases in Greece which decided the Battle of Actium, before it was even fought.

Shakespeare passes swiftly over the next series of events in which Octavia played a major role as pacifier, persuading her husband to be patient with Caesar, who twice asked him for help against Pompey. Antony himself needed men for his Parthian enterprise and so in 37BC the Treaty of Tarentum renewed the triumvirate, and was cynically sealed by the betrothal of Antyllus, aged nine, Antony's eldest son, to Julia, the two-year-old daughter of Caesar. Shakespeare makes Antony's farewell moving: this is the last time he will see Octavia. Much in their real lives happens before the finality of Actium. Antony, now moving against Parthia, once again summons Cleopatra to him at Antioch, in Syria, but we hear nothing from Shakespeare of what must have been a deeply emotional reunion. In exchange for their renewed association he extends her revenues and lands northwards so that she can obtain the cedarwood needed to build the ships required for their new navy. Antony had been compelled to get help from either his unreliable, menacing rival Caesar, with the family connections provided by the worthy but unglamorous Octavia, or from Cleopatra with her greater and more certain wealth. She was in addition, of course, the mother of his twins, and, anyhow, had 'witchcraft in her lips' (*Henry V* V.2). Shakespeare simplified this dilemma by completely cutting the terrible Parthian campaign, and by doing so removing our understanding of the fact that if he had won it Antony would have made himself indisputably more powerful than Caesar. The supreme military glory, which was the motivating ambition of all leading Romans, and the incalculable wealth assured by victory over Rome's arch-enemy Parthia, were worth the huge risks and responsibilities now undertaken by Antony, with Cleopatra's active cooperation. So, before returning to Alexandria to bear Antony's third child, Cleopatra marched with him to the Euphrates to see her Osiris lead the finest Roman army ever assembled, into the East, upon whose victory they had staked everything.

Antony penetrated well into Media, but then through treachery lost his vital siege weapons in the baggage train, after which he could only retreat against the oncoming winter and constant attack. It was a brave and brilliant withdrawal, which only he could have achieved, but with the appalling loss of forty per cent of his army, a crippling disaster. Shakespeare telescopes two years of history now in the twenty-three-line exchange of news between Eros and Enobarbus (III.5), introduced to prepare us for their future and significant roles. Caesar removes Lepidus for intriguing with Pompey, who is then defeated by Agrippa, and then executed, apparently on Antony's orders, for plotting with the Parthians. It is now the year 35BC, and Antony re-establishes his court in Alexandria, from where in the spring he swoops into the East again, capturing the King of Media and his treasure in a clear victory, which he celebrates in a great procession, as Dionysus, victoriously bringing liberation and salvation to Alexandria. Shakespeare refers in passing to this (III.6.35), but concentrates instead understandably, on the fantastic ceremony of the Donations of the Kingdom, as the key reason for Caesar's declaration of war against Cleopatra (not Antony). This Shakespeare also omits, just hinting at war in lines 38 and 85. Caesar's growing self-importance is revealed in this scene in all his balanced speeches, in the speed with which he has dealt with Antony's accusations, and the efficiency of his spies:

> 'I have eyes upon him,
> And his affairs come to me on the wind' (ll.62-3)

as he tells the deserted Octavia. This is confirmed in the next scene by his sudden appearance reported north of Actium, unknown before to Antony's military security system. But the Donations are so spectacular that their rhythmic description by Caesar, coloured by his resentment, loads the scene with its true significance. For him they represent Antony's clear declaration of his complete alliance with Cleopatra, in what was a public religious ceremony, in honour of the god Julius Caesar.

Thus was Antony confirming his aim to carry on Alexander the Great's policy that easterners should and could best rule the East, a belief foreign to Rome and a threat to Octavius. Antony as the incarnation of Dionysus-Osiris was the divine consort of Isis-Cleopatra for the Greeks *and* the Egyptians, and it was under his authority as still being one of the triumvirs that the Donations were announced for the Romans. On his decree, also, the gold coins were issued, in this year 34BC, displaying and naming Antyllus, his eldest Roman son, as his official heir. The Donations were for the Egyptian children only, while the Roman boy, Fulvia's son, is unmistakably recognised as Marcus Antonius Junior, next in Roman law, and so a further threat to Caesar. By this Antony makes it clear that he is still in control, these meticulously planned international relationships confirming that he was not just a jocular general but a strategist of the highest order.

This must have been one of the happiest periods enjoyed by the royal family, until Caesar's provocative replies to Antony convinced him that he must return from the east, where he was again preparing war against the Parthians, and possibly to divert this action against Caesar. The bitterness of Rome's anti-Cleopatra campaign now provoked her to persuade Antony to divorce Octavia, thus allowing the cynical Caesar to declare the queen 'the Enemy of Rome'.

However, in spite of Caesar's propaganda and his own absence from Rome, Antony's support there was still surprisingly strong, a measure of his persistent popularity. No less that three hundred senators and both the consuls for the year 32BC sailed over from Italy to join their triumvir, who, with Cleopatra, was preparing in the port of Ephesus for the great confrontation, which was now inevitable. Not since the Great Alexander had the entire sea-power of the eastern world been in the hands of one man. All this must remind us of the extraordinary proportions of these two romantic figures in the classical landscape, who were able to command such respect, affection, loyalty and hope from both East and West. Antony moved his forces to Patras, Cleopatra ever at his side, which Enobarbus strongly criticised (III.7.10) but Canidius as strongly defended. Both these attitudes Shakespeare toned down because he still needed Enobarbus dramatically, whereas in history he deserted *before* the battle of Actium.

So far the conduct of the principals has been understandable and acceptable, but in flying from Actium, the play asserts, they both abandoned their honour as well, Cleopatra thus adding cowardice to the charge of harlotry and Antony desertion to sexual obsession. This has been invaluable for Roman propaganda, and for historians and dramatists, but fact and reason will have it otherwise. The truth is that their action was a withdrawal planned in advance; this is proved first by the retaining on board of the ships's masts and sails, which in such battles were invariably left ashore, and secondly, by the loading of the queen's vast treasure aboard the flagship. As Caesar swiftly descended from the north and Agrippa had taken Patras and other linking bases south of Actium, Antony realised that he was trapped. To move northeastward and fight it out by land would mean leaving Cleopatra behind with her navy to break out of the blockade by herself, which Antony was not prepared to do. So together they planned to burst out of the bay, through Caesar's lines, and to be followed at a given signal by all those ships that could disengage themselves. However, time and the late afternoon breeze were against them. In only thirty-six urgent lines (III.10) Shakespeare recounts the action as it would have appeared to the amazed and horrified Enobarbus and Scarus on shore, joined then by Candidius, to explain his army's desertions to Caesar. Two examples of how the playwright condenses and embroiders the facts are the excuses of Canidius, and then Enobarbus: 'six kings already/Show me the way of yielding', and 'I'll follow/the wounded chance of Antony, though my reason sits in the wind against me' (33-6). There is defeated justification in the softness of the first, and rich economy and a natural continuance of the sea battle in the metaphors of Enobarbus.

For Antony, the disaster was, indeed, only a 'wounded chance', a lost sea-fight, but by no means the end of the war, which now had to be fought from Egypt, which was still rich and free. Shakespeare contracts the time again, because Caesar had army mutinies and other troubles of his own to settle in Italy, for which he needed money, as always. So eleven months were to pass before he could finally get his hands on Cleopatra's gold.

Shakespeare has so far used three acts to cover eleven years and now devotes as many as seventeen scenes to show us the tragedy of the last days of the lovers. On landing on the Libyan coast, Antony found that his African army had deserted, but he remained there with two faithful friends, for a month, while Cleopatra hurried to reach Alexandria before the news of the disaster. Antony's offer to help his followers to get away to Corinth is effectively used, as is the farewell to his servants, along with Cleopatra's despatch of Caesarion with part of her navy across the desert to the Red Sea, in readiness for an eastward retreat, if necessary. Both Antony's envoys, Antyllus, his fourteen-year-old son, and then Euphronius, the children's tutor, were rejected by Caesar. However, when he learnt that the queen had transferred her treasures to the mausoleum, with means to burn them, he sent the unlucky Thidias to beguile her into betraying Antony. Shakespeare makes the most of this vivid scene, clothing the queen's repartee in an uncertainty as to her loyalty, but retaining our sympathies for both of the lovers. Cleopatra's mention of her birthday after their most bitter quarrel is a masterly piece of restraint to contrast with Antony's loud protestations of his renewed valour, which are too much for Enobarbus (III.13.199).

Enobarbus

Enobarbus 'earns a place i' th'story' (III.13.46) not because he leaves Antony but because he speaks the supreme descriptive passage in all Shakespeare, giving the essence of the woman who was the most exciting of all Shakespeare's female characters. Although he is a soldier and Antony's lieutenant, he is also his companion, adviser and friend, what in fact the first Ptolemy was to Alexander, with privileges which permit him to tell the truth, to criticise, even to be familiar, and never to flatter, which both Antony and the queen must have welcomed.

We learn from his first two speeches that he has authority in the court, calls the queen simply Cleopatra (a fact mentioned by Plutarch), enjoys wine, and looks to the future. Later in this scene his blunt and cynical exchanges with Antony reveal a surprising intimacy in his knowledge of his women, and particularly his deep understanding of Cleopatra's behaviour and her sincere love. He has an easy freedom in his prose style, accentuated by Antony's consistent responses in verse.

Enobarbus shows the small respect he has for all the triumvirs in the Treaty scene (II.2), insisting to Lepidus that he will not try to control Antony's conduct towards Caesar, being facetious about Fulvia, and utterly cynical about their hypocrisy (ll.107–10), which provokes the reprimand from Antony: 'Thou art a soldier only; speak no more'. His fearless but impertinent reply, 'That truth should be silent I had almost forgot', also offends Caesar (l.117). He is present on all important occasions. After Misenum (II.6), having defended his General from the provoking insinuations of Pompey about Cleopatra, he acts as a narrator and gossipy commentator to the pirate Menas on Antony's new marriage, in which he certainly has no confidence (l.117), foretelling that his return to his 'Egyptian dish' will cause disaster, since Antony 'married but his occasion' there. On the galley he not only proposes 'Ha, my brave Emperor' (II.7.96), which words must have infuriated Caesar, but he leads the final song and dance.

Always the keen observer, Enobarbus is made to cut through all superficial falsities, revealing as well as his own character those of the persons he talks to and about. This is evident, when he is with Agrippa (II.2); they make fun of the flattery by Lepidus of their masters, and mock the sincerity of their tears at parting. He is realistic, too, in the recognition that with Lepidus out of the way the other two will 'grind one the other' (III.5.14). He shares three brief dialogues with Cleopatra: before Actium, when he strongly opposes her insistence with Antony on fighting at sea (III.7), after the tragedy which he firmly blames on her (III.13.1–11), and in the scene when standing apart, puzzled, they watch and comment on Antony's touching farewell to the servants (IV.2.13–24), which makes even Enobarbus, the tough campaigner, weep, 'an ass, onion-eyed'. His horror at Cleopatra's flight is such that he cannot bear to watch, and must be told by Scarus of Antony's pursuit; yet he leaves all criticism to Scarus and Canidius (III.10). But soon he speaks his doubts aloud: 'mine honesty and I begin to square', in four consecutive asides, causing Antony to share his belief in Cleopatra's possible betrayal with Thidias (III.13.62). His thoughts of his own desertion are clearly expressed in the last 'Tis better playing with a lion's whelp [Caesar] than with an old one dying' (ll.93–4). In Caesar's camp he is alone now, and dies repentant after three soliloquies (IV.6.9). Thus this practical, unsentimental, wise man of the world, so critical of everyone else, has by his desertion of his trusting friend in his extreme need committed the worst crime in the play. Shakespeare has used him as a common-sensical but very personal equivalent to a Chorus, to reveal through his honesty the swift action of the story, the motives and personalities of all involved with himself.

The placing of the mystical scene (IV.3) of the departure of Hercules and his revellers to Caesar's camp, between Antony's gloomy farewell and the lovers' most intimate interlude in the whole play, reveals the author's special skill. Coming before that of Enobarbus, the god's abandonment will disturb us even more when we know that according to familiar legend this had happened before the falls of the other great cities: Troy, Athens and Jerusalem. But Antony is allowed one more victory before his agonies of the fleet's desertion, and then Cleopatra's reported death, which swiftly force him to his own triumph over defeat, to 'stand up peerless' and 'make the ghosts gaze' (I.1.39; IV.14.52).

Caesar and Cleopatra

Now comes the last round. The irony that it was Gaius Proculeius, recommended as trustworthy by Antony, who with Gallus captures the queen, is not stressed. This Cornelius Gallus was the poet and new general of Antony's defected African army, left by Caesar as his governor of Egypt. With their help Caesar had got hold of both the queen and her gold, with which he could now pay off his armies, since the civil war was over. Did they actually ever meet, these two enemies of circumstance? Both of them supreme egotists, crafty and far-thinking statesmen, ruthless in the rat-race of survival (Cleopatra had insisted on her sister's being executed, although Julius Caesar had spared her), they were well matched. But Cleopatra, with Antony dead and now totally in Caesar's power, fell ill, anxious above all for her threatened children, mentioned only briefly (V.2.131, 202). But Shakespeare decided to get the most, dramatically, out of their meeting, leaving us to admire and interpret for ourselves the battle of their wits. Each believes the other to have been fooled and so they part satisfied.

Cleopatra, who had caused Caesar ceaseless worry ever since his great-uncle's death, committed suicide, probably much to his relief, on 1 August 30BC, twelve days after his arrival in her capital. The exact cause of her death was not established, but the serpent legend was apt, the poetic asp taking over from the cobra, the Egyptian snake goddess seen clearly in the royal diadem of the Pharaohs, continued in use by the Ptolemies, and so by the queen at her death. In Caesar's triumph two snakes were shown on her statue, as the Goddess Isis. The serpent was sacred to Isis, and was believed to confer immortality by its bite. But Cleopatra, being both a Pharaoh and Isis, was already immortal during her life, a legend which has since been confirmed both by the asp and by Shakespeare.

Caius Julius Caesar and Octavius Augustus

Caesar celebrated that important August. of 30BC by assuming the title Augustus with the role of Emperor three years later in 27BC, at the youthful age of thirty-six. Shakespeare has been developing him subtly from his first words, as readers of *Julius Caesar* (IV.1.2) will recall. Although the youngest member of the triumvirate, he insists upon the death of the brother of Lepidus, arguing with Antony, as though with an equal, right up to his final victory over all others at Alexandria. Julius must have divined seeds of greatness in the unremarkable youth to have chosen him as his adopted son and heir, for it was this unique chance that gave him the spur to achieve fame. He was about to test him in the great Parthian wars, for which he was being prepared with Agrippa at Apollonia in March 44BC, when Brutus struck. Octavius, closely observing Caesar's climb to and grip on power, had noted how he had achieved it with single-minded determination and with armies. He added to these a merciless exploitation of all men, women and means, at the easy expense of his conscience and moral integrity. This needed patience, pretence and courage, putting politics always before personal pleasure, as the possessor of time, the master of opportunity.

For his revenge he used Antony as Caesar's friend and the best soldier of his time to defeat Brutus and Cassius, and then Sextus Pompey. Lepidus, who was Caesar's successor as High Priest, he used diplomatically, but at the most suitable moment disgraced him and took over his two legions, and third share of the empire. He shamelessly used his wives and his sister Octavia to guarantee treaties and alliances, only so long as he could keep or acquire more power. The first great Caesar had died because he was merciful and forgave his enemies, notably Brutus and Cassius, so Octavius made no such mistake, executing all who had opposed or might still threaten him, if spared. His pitiless post-war conduct at Modena, Perugia, Philippi and Alexandria confirmed this. Shakespeare suggests all these qualities throughout the play in the tightly packed speeches: the controlled, cold, impersonal, assured, selfish superiority, which contrast so obviously with the warmth and impetuous generosity of both Antony and Cleopatra. Each of these alone was a formidable enough enemy: Antony as the superior soldier and most popular statesman, Cleopatra as the mother of his rival Caesarion, and queen of the fabulously wealthy Egypt, so allied together they demanded the total concentration and exercise of his strongest weapon—his utter efficiency. When Alexandrian revels delayed Antony's military aid Caesar could hypocritically fan the flames of Rome's condemnation of the gypsy queen, although he was self-indulgently immoral himself, and far more faithless than Antony. Antony's divorce of Octavia, possibly already planned by Octavius as he joined them in marriage, and his liberal international policies for the rule of the eastern kingdoms by the Ptolemies, so clearly displayed in the Disposals, were all welcome ammunition for his untiring anti-Cleopatra propaganda. So when Agrippa's brilliant tactics on both sea and land before Actium trapped Antony into proving his love for Cleopatra by following her to Egypt Caesar must have rejoiced. Antony had to die; preferably by his own or the queen's action. So once in Alexandria, with no more to fear, Caesar could enjoy the discomfort of the lovers, first Antony and then Cleopatra, in the agony of their defeats. Wise Shakespeare makes even his oration, for such it was, at Antony's death seem punctuated by excuses and self-glorifications, so that the stiff compliments really sound false. And he is even shown obliged to justify his pursuit of Antony in the war by displaying his 'writings' to his subordinates. From his vantage as conqueror he could risk, even enjoy, a meeting with the degraded and distraught queen, and her final betrayal, apparently by her treasurer, Seleucus.

But she entered willingly into 'the secret house of death', welcoming its stroke 'as a lover's pinch, which hurts, and is desired', like Antony who said:

> But I will be
> A bridegroom in my death, and run into't
> As to a lover's bed. (IV.14.100)

Now Caesar could afford to be generous to her, and perhaps even admire the bravery of her suicide: 'O noble weakness'. This relieved him of the danger, from public reaction, of dragging her through a Roman triumph and then from the dilemma of whether, as was customary afterwards, to execute her. So he had it announced that he had called in the snake-charmers to try to save her, and that she could be buried together with Antony in the completed mausoleum, as they had wished, in Alexandria. Because of its splendour and its great founder he spared the city, but not the unfortunate Caesarion, nor Antyllus, who were speedily executed, Canidius also. But Agrippa, whose talents had brought Caesar successfully to Egypt, became consul, and married first the daughter of Antony and Octavia, and then, under compulsion, Julia, the daughter of the Emperor Caesar Augustus, who was to rule for more than forty years until his death in 14AD, when he was poisoned by his last wife. But he proved his words in the play (IV.6.5), and brought 'the time of universal peace', when the . . . 'world shall bear the olive freely', and Egypt became a Roman province under the personal care of the Emperor. Augustus, too, was made a god and joined those other three immortals: his great-uncle, Antony, and Cleopatra.

General note of advice

The student should read these notes thoroughly before reading the text of the play. Then he should read the text straight through without stopping to clarify every unfamiliar word or problem of meaning. A second, slower reading should then be carried out, in detail, referring carefully to the notes in the text, and once again to the relevant sections of this volume.

Wherever he may be the student should do his best to go to see the play performed by any group, either professional or amateur; he should also arrange to try and see any of the films which exist of the plays *Julius Caesar, Caesar and Cleopatra* and *Antony and Cleopatra*.

To borrow recordings on discs, tapes or cassettes is essential. Students will be able to get helpful advice on how to achieve all these suggestions in connection with all the works of Shakespeare from any office, centre, library, or Institute of the British Council.

The suggestions for further reading (Part 5 of these notes) should be followed. As many as possible of the listed titles should be consulted and read. Other books and articles, not only about this play but about Shakespeare, his other works, and the periods of history concerned, can be found in literary journals and reference books.

Part 4

Hints for study

Points for detailed study

There are five elements which may be considered to comprise the student's perception of the work:

(1) History, the known facts.
(2) Plutarch's selection of these, and North's translations of them into *The Lives*.
(3) Shakespeare's version, and his translation of this into poetic drama.
(4) The personal interpretations of these three by (*i*) the authors, editors, and critics whose views the student may read, (*ii*) the directors of the plays and films he may see and hear, and (*iii*) teachers.
(5) Finally, the student's own assessment of (1) to (3), with or without (4). This will be of most value to those for whom the student is working on the play.

To consider Shakespeare's reasons for creating the play the student has the introductory section of this book, and the recommended text, to provide the following:

(1) Shakespeare's personal and professional backgrounds.
(2) The range and sequence of the plays and his interest in historical and Roman dramas.
(3) The period in his career when this play was written.
(4) That he did not write for profit only, but for the expression of his delight in words.
(5) And, in this play, his new-found reconciliation between the demands and the joy of love.
(6) In short, that he wrote the play to show the power of love: a love so strong that by self-sacrifice it could triumph nobly in death over the selfish, material rewards of worldly success.

Themes and characters

The student will notice a number of contrasting and overlapping themes which Shakespeare chooses to accentuate and weave into the main one of *love*, proposed above:

(*i*) loyalty/betrayal,
(*ii*) love/duty,
(*iii*) Egypt/Rome,
(*iv*) power/glory,
(*v*) the decline and fall of the Roman Antony.

Different kinds of love have the power to create the motives of the characters, who by their words, attitudes and actions provide the themes.

(i) Loyalty/betrayal

Loyalty is faith to a lover, friend or master, betrayal is the result of insufficient love. Varying degrees of this strength of love are shown by the five principals in the play towards each other, and by followers to their masters.

The loyalties of Antony, Cleopatra, Octavia, Enobarbus and Caesar are tested and shown in different scenes. Enobarbus, Octavius, Proculeius and Seleucus fail in their loyalty to the lovers, while Eros, Charmian and Iras succeed. But loyalty to one will be betrayal of another. Thus Antony's Egyptian loyalty to Cleopatra was his betrayal of Roman Antony and Octavius, by failing in his duty. The desertion of Enobarbus was later turned back to loyalty to Antony, by his death. But Eros and the ladies-in-waiting, by their deaths, acted out of pure loyalty to those whom they devotedly served.

(ii) and (iii) Love/duty; Egypt/Rome

These simplified headings represent, first, Cleopatra: her allure, her court, wealth and power—they are all Egypt. In contrast against them are Roman Antony, his Roman wives, his duties as triumvir, ally and hero of Rome, and Caesar, his grim, efficient determination to win his inheritance and the world.

(iv) Power/glory

These can represent the worldly powers of Julius Caesar, Cleopatra, Antony and Octavius; and the loving power of Antony and Cleopatra against the material power of Caesar, which leads to their glory in death.

The extremes of all these headings are stressed for contrast throughout and then balanced against each other, for example gods/humans; war/love: peace/life/death.

(v) The decline and fall of the Roman Antony

This was caused, mainly, by Julius Caesar (his death), Cleopatra, Fulvia, Octavia, Caesar (Rome), and, of course, Antony himself. But Shakespeare's theme is not the helplessness of man in front of fate, nor Antony's fall through lust, it is rather the power of love to achieve final honour.

The individual personalities of the characters are revealed by their speeches, which explain their reputations, motives and actions.

The student should refer to the summaries in Part 2 of these Notes, and then the commentaries on the scenes and the characters. By examining for example, the first three scenes in Alexandria, he will notice how the playwright has shown through the Queen's words and actions her less likeable qualities: her arguing, demanding, mockery and deceit (I.1,2,3). These failings are then counter-balanced by the assurances of Enobarbus (I.2.136) to Antony of her true love, by Antony's patience, and by her own sudden mellowing farewell (I.3.96). Then comes the powerful revelation of her passion and yearning for the absent Antony (I.5), before the contrast of her violence to the messenger, five scenes later, on hearing of his marriage (II.5).

This procedure will reveal Shakespeare's planning and constructive method of scene placing for maximum effect, and should be followed throughout for all the characters.

We notice the skill with which the poet reinforces the personalities of the two principals through criticism or praise of both those who are with or opposed to them. Thus, in the barge scene, the praises of Enobarbus are amplified by the admitted admiration of Cleopatra's enemies, Caesar's two chief ministers (II.2.188). Similar examples can be found for Antony before and after his death. But naturally the most potent and convincing opinions will be those of the lovers themselves, which are increasingly built up in the last two acts, when all recriminations are over, and the bitter desire for death must be justified, and made possible by the conviction of the infinity of their love. It is in Acts IV and V that Shakespeare's inspired imagination, by the repeated use of strikingly evocative images and figures of speech, compels us to accept the truth of their loves, and the nobility of their suicides.

Quotations

To quote original words and phrases is to confirm the exactness and authority of the language, and quotation is also useful to illustrate and reinforce opinions and discussions. This play is so rich that almost every speech contains some quotable descriptive word or phrase. It will be more rewarding for the student to gather to his memory short adjectival associations for characters and atmosphere than to try to retain and reproduce large passages of the verse.

Language affects hearers and readers differently according to the private images which the words evoke in their minds.

The effect may be achieved and made memorable by (*i*) An unusual, apt, or striking adjective, qualifying a surprising, metaphorical noun, or (*ii*) simply: the order, the sound, the rhythm and the colour of the phrase, as, for instance, in

> Age cannot wither her, nor custom stale
> Her infinite variety: . . . (II.2.238)

That is to say that Cleopatra is eternal not only in her physical aspect, her persistent youth, but in her constantly exciting and limitless intellectual and emotional diversity. Antony's care for his appearance, his masculinity and age are expressed, for example, in the quotations concerning his hair: 'being barbered ten times o'er' (II.2.237), 'this grizzled head' (III.13.16), the 'curled Antony' (V.2.297). But after Actium he had used his hair to illustrate his shame:

> My very hairs do mutiny, for the white
> Reprove the brown for rashness and they them . . ., (III.11.13)

Throughout the commentaries in Part 2, frequent use of quotations has been made to describe characters, motives and situations because the play abounds in the forcefully affectionate or critical comments of, and about, the lovers, which lead from one novel image to another.

For example, Cleopatra's reference, hopefully, to her absent Antony as 'murmuring, "Where's my serpent of Old Nile?"' (a much-quoted phrase in I.5.25), starts off a sequence of images and associations concerning snakes, flowing throughout (see Lepidus's lines in II.7) to the Clown's 'the pretty worm of Nilus' (V.2.244), the Queen's 'Have I aspic on my lips?', as Iras dies at her kiss, then lastly to her, now the dying mother's

> Dost thou not see the baby at my breast
> That sucks the nurse asleep? (l.305)

Other themes made easily quotable by the rich clusters of imagery around them are:

(1) The world, mentioned here no less than forty-two times
(2) Egypt and the East, heat, luxury, fertility
(3) The heavens, the gods, the supernatural, oriental mystery
(4) Water: sea, rivers, wine, liquids and melting.

For example note how Shakespeare echoes Antony's prediction of his fall, when Cleopatra, his 'terrene moon', is eclipsed (III.13.152) by the queen's words at his death:

> *The crown o' the earth* doth melt. My Lord. (Antony dies)
> *O withered is the garland of the war,*
> The soldier's pole is fallen, *young boys and girls*
> *Are level now with men. The odds is gone*
> And *there is nothing left remarkable*
> *Beneath the visting moon.* (IV.15.63)

Words and phrases italicised are well-known quotations now. We see how the death of the 'greatest soldier' on earth makes, naturally, the military metaphors flood out, and 'melt' away, leaving Cleopatra nothing 'left remarkable' to live for. They had 'kissed away kingdoms' (III.10.7) because they had remained true to their 'finest part of true love' (I.2.137), and, as Cleopatra proclaimed, once:

> Eternity was in our lips and eyes
> Bliss in our brows' bent: none our parts so poor
> But was a race of heaven. (I.3.35)

Recommended passages

The following speeches are recommended for special study, their language being notably rich in imagery, and so quotation.

I.2.128–58: Enobarbus, in prose about Cleopatra
I.5.18–38: Cleopatra about Antony
II.1.19–38: Pompey about Cleopatra and Antony
II.2.93–102: Antony; 188–245: Enobarbus on Cleopatra (Cydnus)
III.10.9–23: Scarus at Actium
III.11.1–24: Antony after Actium
III.13.4–12, 29–37: Enobarbus; 110–131: Antony about Cleopatra
III.13.157–200: Antony, Cleopatra, Enobarbus
IV.6.29–35; 11.12–23: Enobarbus in soliloquy
IV.12.9–49: Antony against Cleopatra after the navy leaves
IV.14.2–20, 39–101: Antony and Eros before the suicide
IV.15.9–90: Antony's death
V.2.1–8, 49–62: Cleopatra, 76–99: her 'Emperor Antony'
    226–32, 276–315: Cleopatra preparing for her death

Model questions

As the play develops the student should, after each scene, be asking himself such questions as: who are these people, why are they speaking like this, what are they hoping and planning to do? Is he correct in his conduct to her, could she have acted otherwise? Why are they here, at this time? What will be the result of their words, discussions and behaviour? How are the speeches holding my interest or giving me pleasure? And, finally, how does what I read in the text confirm the high reputation of the play?

Examination questions, although phrased differently, involve these queries, and so the student should apply them all to this play. Then he should acquire experience in formulating written replies, as examples, to the following:

(1) How does Cleopatra change from 'wrangling Queen' to 'lass unparalleled', after the battle of Actium?
(2) Why is Enobarbus vital to the play?
(3) How does the author maintain our sympathies for the lovers, in spite of their actions?
(4) 'Cleopatra, not Antony, is Caesar's enemy.' Discuss.
(5) 'Loyalty commands the play from start to finish.' How?
(6) 'Not to sympathise with Antony would be to take sides against poetry.' Discuss.
(7) Was Antony's marriage to Octavia a help to him or not?
(8) 'The play is a study of Mars and Venus.' Discuss.
(9) Queen or courtesan? 'Emperor Antony' or 'amorous surfeiter'? How justified were Rome's criticisms?
(10) How is the scene on Pompey's galley significant?
(11) We 'that trade in love', admits Cleopatra. Consider this and Octavia in the themes of love and empire.
(12) How are the climates of Rome and Egypt emphasised on two different levels?
(13) 'Caesar must not only be in the right, but must keep proving he is.' Discuss.
(14) What are the purposes of the scenes involving: the messengers, Ventidius, Thidias, Seleucus, the Clown?
(15) How do Charmian and Iras, and the poetry, add to the drama in the final scene?

Some suggested answers

'The play is the peak of Shakespeare's poetic achievement.' Is it tragedy or love story, drama or literature?

Antony and Cleopatra can be called all of these. Critics have praised the play highly for its magnificent poetry. This becomes clearer to us in the last two acts devoted to the suicides of the 'royal pair'. Their reasons for deciding to take their lives raise the level from domestic and political contention to noble, even divine drama. But before this we have noticed a compact richness in the poetry of the speeches, for there are no long sombre soliloquies here, as in *Hamlet* or *Macbeth*, but brisk dialogues infused with such power and double, sometimes triple, meanings that we can forgive Shakespeare any problems of comprehension for the pleasure which the sound, colours and vitality of the images provoke. The succeeding words reveal to us simultaneously the progress of the struggle, the motives of the combatants and the personalities of the speakers, but in a procession of metaphors, similes and surprising imagery excelled nowhere else by the playwright.

Shakespeare, a craftsman of the theatre and a man of affairs, was first of all a poet and in phrase after eloquent phrase he astonishes us with their originality and complete suitability. Here are some, for example: 'a strange invisible perfume', 'infinite variety', 'marble constant', 'delicious poison', 'Royal wench', 'A Roman thought', 'High-battled Caesar', 'the ebb'd man', 'the tunéd spheres', 'fall not a tear', 'the morn-dew on the myrtle leaf', 'man of men', 'our lamp is spent', 'we are for the dark', 'her strong toil of grace'.

That Antony and Cleopatra loved each other and had children, was their love story. That they loved too well, and unwisely, was their tragedy. That their motives for universal East-West peace and happiness clashed with Caesar's design for his secure Roman Empire provided the drama. That Shakespeare, then, was inspired to create a new 'wonderful piece of work' from North's version of the Antony and Cleopatra legend, by his own imaginative genius has made the play into a monument of literature. Shakespeare's 'vague hospitality' invites us all to share his generous poetic banquet but specially to interpret and enjoy the 'Egyptian dishes' on their Roman 'trenchers', each in his own way.

Do you agree that 'in *Antony and Cleopatra* no persons are bad'?

A statement such as this compels us to consider both the play and history, and the conclusion then reached confirms Shakespeare's great liking for humankind. For he chooses to do without villains, in his story of the lovers' fight against Caesar and the might of Rome, in order to retain their half of the world. All three were ambitious, and ambition must be made of stern stuff if it is to succeed. But Shakespeare makes their particular actions, which might be called bad, acceptable by causing us to share, and so sympathise with, their motives. Antony's neglect of Rome, which is insulting and irresponsible to Caesar, and even the divorce of Octavia, so serious for them all, are made comprehensible for us by the strength of Cleopatra's love. Cleopatra's taunts and tricks are an essential part of her deep, loving character but, we realise, are also caused by the fear and despair of a statesmanlike queen and mother, who depends upon Antony to retain her kingdom safe for her heirs.

Caesar, cold, hard and humourless, even when celebrating with Sextus Pompey on his galley, may be unattractive, and his actions may be harsh, but they are reasonable for a man determined to rule the entire Roman world, when provoked and challenged by a rival such as Antony.

Enobarbus is guilty of desertion, but only when he realises that Antony's 'wounded chance' is beyond saving. He can see 'a diminution in our captain's brain' and 'when valour preys on reason, it eats the sword it fights with'. Moreover, when the master he leaves is so generous and forgiving and Caesar so thankless, he pays for his 'infamous revolt', for his heart will 'break to powder' in the bravery of his death.

To Caesar the behaviour of both Antony and Cleopatra is bad, because they are the enemies of Rome and also his personal enemies. To Antony, Cleopatra's apparent betrayals make him believe the worst, and that she is a witch. Her final lie to him, in sending news of her death, is the most bitter of all because it drives him to take his own life. But this he forgives, as Cleopatra forgives Caesar, for allowing her to make him an 'Ass, unpolicied' by strengthening her own determination to die. So, too, Caesar's last, forgiving tributes to the lovers are generous. He says that 'the death of Antony is not a single' death, for 'in the name lay a moiety [half] of the world'. Cleopatra he described as

> Bravest at the last,
> She levelled at our purposes, and being royal
> Took her own way. (V.2.332–4)

How does Shakespeare's use of special language enrich his descriptions of the main characters?

By the time he wrote this play around 1606–7, Shakespeare had become brilliantly skilful in his use of metaphors and similes, that is, describing one thing in terms of another, or as being like another. In *Antony and Cleopatra* he prefers to give his personages short paragraphs of conversation rather than long passages to speak to themselves, which are called soliloquies. But the exchanges, which may be of between five to ten lines each, are tightly packed with these figures of speech, verbal pictures painted by the ingenious use of the right words to arouse fresh, unusual associations.

For example, Cleopatra hopes that the absent Antony thinks of her as smooth and sinuous, his 'serpent of old Nile', and later describes

herself as 'a morsel for a monarch'. This idea of Cleopatra as food is
continued by Enobarbus when he says that Antony will not be able to
resist returning to his 'Egyptian dish'. Antony refers to her as many
different things according to his moods, such as, in anger, 'a right
gypsy', or, in affection, as 'the armourer of his heart', when he leaves
'like a man of steel' for the battle. On his victorious return she is 'this
great fairy', and 'thou day of the world'. Shakespeare uses the word
'world' forty-two times, more than in any other play, and by doing so
encourages us to remember that the drama is for the world and is en-
acted by its most powerful political players. Antony is described within
the first twelve lines of the play as 'the triple-pillar of the world', and
then by Cleopatra as 'the demi-Atlas', whose noble face would command 'the worship of the world', and when he is dying he is her 'crown
o' the earth', in whose death, says Caesar, 'lay a moiety of the world'.

Caesar is described in the course of the play, usually by Antony, as
'scarce-bearded', 'the boy', the 'young Roman boy', 'this novice', then
as 'blossoming Caesar', who when victorious wears the 'rose of youth',
and, as 'universal landlord' to Cleopatra, is 'Sole sir o' th'world'. So
the wheel of fortune has turned and Caesar is on top, but Cleopatra is
'marble constant' in her resolve to die. Dying, she describes herself as
'fire and air', and as she goes Charmian aptly calls her 'O Eastern star',
because the morning star is also Venus, the goddess of love. As Charmian closes the 'downy window' (eyes) of her Eastern queen she gives
her the last, very famous description, which sums up exactly what
Cleopatra has been beneath her robe and crown: 'a lass unparalleled',
a girl beyond compare.

Do you agree that 'Death is kind in this play'?

The deaths which we hear about and see are those of Fulvia, Enobarbus,
Eros, Charmian, Iras, Antony and Cleopatra. And, certainly, Shakespeare implies that all seven are made noble by dying, because their
actions have led them to their ends on behalf of others. All die, really,
for Antony, and he dies for Cleopatra. Fulvia, Antony's first wife, dies
as a result of the failure of her revolt against Caesar, which she bravely
made in order to attract her husband back to Rome from Cleopatra.
And she succeeds, but too late, so that Antony only realises her true
value when '. . . she's good being gone'. This idea remains in Shakespeare's mind to be repeated two scenes later in Caesar's complaint that
'the ebbed man' is not loved 'till ne'er worth love, comes dear by being
lacked'.

Enobarbus, realising that he cannot serve Caesar against such a
generous master, is compelled to die, and so return to Antony. It was
Enobarbus who said earlier:

> he that can endure
> To follow with allegiance a fall'n lord
> Does conquer him that did his master conquer,
> And earns a place in the story.

The self-sacrifice of Eros is made greater but pathetic by its uselessness, and yet Antony's unsoldierly incompetence in his last killing (of himself) allows us to suffer with the queen at his death, and be moved by their words which precede it.

Mardian's words to Antony giving the false account of Cleopatra's death are prophetic, because she did die calling to him, his name 'was divided between her heart and lips: she rendered life/Thy name so buried in her'. And in Mardian's final confirmation of her death,

ANTONY: Dead then?
MARDIAN:　　　Dead.

the single, short and terrible word, a repetition of Antony's own monosyllable describing Fulvia's death to Enobarbus, is like an assassin's rifle shot, and it is fatal to Antony. But it sparks off in Shakespeare's mind a succession of beautiful images which continue to accompany both the lovers through the doors of the 'secret house' of death out into the bright land beyond, 'where souls do couch on flowers' and 'immortal longings' are satisfied. For this is Egypt, the land of the Pyramids and tomb monuments, such as that in which Cleopatra dies, the land of life after death, where, we must not forget, Antony was Osiris and Cleopatra his wife Isis, and, as gods, both were immortal. So Antony realises that with her death 'the torch is out', 'the long day's task is done, and we must sleep', just as loyal Charmian, in the last scene of all, says to the queen,

> Finish, good lady, the bright day is done,
> And we are for the dark.

But the thought of sleep is only temporary for Antony.. He must not stay uselessly alive but 'will o'ertake' Cleopatra. Begging her to wait for him he says 'I come my Queen', 'I will be a bridegroom in my death, and run into't [his sword] as to a lover's bed.' Since this is a play about mutual passion Shakespeare boldly continues this vivid idea, confident that even in her death Cleopatra will, characteristically, have such elemental desires that she can describe the snake's bite as

> 'The stroke of death is as a lover's pinch
> Which hurts, and is desired.'

So Death is, indeed, kind here, because it leads those who embrace it willingly, and so bravely removing its sting, to a chance of grace and glory.

Part 5

Suggestions for further reading

The text

New Swan Shakespeare, Advanced Series, *Antony and Cleopatra*. Edited by John Ingledew, Longman, London, 1971. This is a first class text

General reading

Criticism

FIEDLER, LESLIE A.: *The Stranger in Shakespeare*, Paladin, London, 1974

KNIGHT, G. WILSON: *The Imperial Theme*, Methuen, London, 1965. Particularly valuable for *Julius Caesar* and *Antony and Cleopatra*

ROWSE, A.L.: *Shakespeare's Sonnets, the Problems Solved*, Macmillan, London, 1973. Ingenious but not the last word on the subject

KNOTT, JAN: *Shakespeare our Contemporary*, Methuen, London, 1972

SPENCER, T.J.B.: 'Antony and Cleopatra', and 'Julius Caesar', in *Shakespeare, The Writer and his Work*, Longmans, London, 1964

SPURGEON, CAROLINE F.E.: *Shakespeare's Imagery*, Cambridge University Press, Cambridge, 1958

Biographies

BURGESS, ANTONY: *Shakespeare*, Penguin Books, Harmondsworth, 1972. Useful and excellently illustrated

BURGESS, ANTONY: *Nothing Like the Sun: A Story of Shakespeare's Love Life*, Heinemann, London, 1964. A novel

GRANT, MICHAEL: *Julius Caesar*, Panther, London, 1972

GRANT, MICHAEL: *Cleopatra*, Panther, London, 1974. Most valuable

SPENCER, T.J.B.: *Shakespeare's Plutarch*, Peregrine, London, 1964

Elizabethan England

ROWSE, A.L.: *The England of Elizabeth*, Cardinal, London, 1973

WILSON, JOHN DOVER: *Life in Shakespeare's England*, Penguin Books, London, 1951

Elizabethan Theatre

BRADBURY, JIM: *Shakespeare and His Theatre*, Longman, London, 1975

NICHOL, ALLARDYCE: *British Drama*, Harrap, London, 1951

The author of these notes

PAUL GOTCH, OBE, was educated at Shrewsbury School and the Central School of Arts and Crafts. He has had a career of teaching and lecturing on English language and literature for the British Council, serving in Greece, Egypt, Turkey, Italy, Spain, Ghana, Iran, Colombia and Lebanon. He was visiting Professor at the University of Alexandria in 1976 and 1977.

Since 1978 Mr Gotch has acted as External Examiner for Trinity College of Music in Speech and Drama, Effective Speaking and Spoken English, in India, Sri Lanka, Singapore, Hong Kong, Australia, Italy, Colombia and New Zealand.

His public lectures *The Influence of the East upon Shakespeare; A Girdle round about the Earth—Shakespeare's Universality*; and *Upon a Midnight Pillow—The Sonnets of Shakespeare* were published in 1973 and 1977.

Mr Gotch is also deeply concerned with archaeology, specially in the Middle East, and his book *Three Caravan Cities* (1946) has been followed by articles in learned journals on discoveries made during his stay in Iran, and his three solo expeditions there afterwards as a surface archaeologist.

From 1978 he has accompanied, as Guest Lecturer on history, art and archaeology, many Swan Hellenic Art Treasure Tours of Persia, Anatolia, Syria, Jordan, The Holy Land and Peru.